Memory and Mission

David C. Steinmetz

Theological Reflections on the Christian Past

Memory and Mission

Abingdon Press
Nashville

MEMORY AND MISSION

Theological Reflections on the Christian Past

Copyright © 1988 by Abingdon Press

This book is printed on acid-free paper.

Library of Congress Cataloging-in-Publication Data

Steinmetz, David Curtis.
  Memory and mission: theological reflections on the
Christian past / David C. Steinmetz.
    p. cm.
  ISBN 0-687-24783-7 (alk. paper)
  1. Church. 2. History (Theology) I. Title.
BV600.2.S76   1988
262—dc19   88-19063
                                                      CIP

Scripture quotations unless otherwise noted are from the
Revised Standard Version of the Bible, copyright 1946, 1952,
1971 by the Division of Christian Education of the National
Council of the Churches of Christ in the USA, and used by
permission.

Scripture quotations noted NIV are from the Holy Bible:
New International Version. Copyright © 1973, 1978, 1984 by
the International Bible Society. Used by permission of
Zondervan Bible Publishers.

COVER & BOOK DESIGN BY JOHN ROBINSON

MANUFACTURED BY THE PARTHENON PRESS AT
NASHVILLE, TENNESSEE, UNITED STATES OF AMERICA

Nine essays appearing in this volume first appeared in the following journals and are reprinted here with the permission of those journals. All have been reedited and some have been rewritten for this volume.

1. "The Necessity of the Past," *Theology Today* 33 (July, 1976), 168-76.
2. "Reformation and Conversion," *Theology Today* 35 (April, 1978), 25-32.
3. "Woe to me if I do not preach the Gospel!" *The Duke Divinity School Review* 39 (1974), 1-9.
4. "The Protestant Minister and the Teaching Office of the Church," *Theological Education* (Spring, 1983), 45-59.
5. "Asbury's Doctrine of Ministry," *The Duke Divinity School Review* 40 (1975), 10-17.
6. "Theological Reflections on the Reformation and the Status of Women," *The Duke Divinity School Review* 41 (1976), 197-207.

7. "Mary Reconsidered," *Christianity Today* 20 (1975), 240-43.
8. "The Superiority of Pre–Critical Exegesis," *Theology Today* 37 (April, 1980), 27-38.
9. "The Making of a Theologian," *Lancaster Theological Seminary Bulletin* 3 (1969), 8-19.

CONTENTS

It is the thesis of this book that memory of the past is essential to the Church's self-identity and thus to its mission. I argue the case for this thesis in some detail in the first essay in this volume. It seems to me that no real purpose would be served by anticipating those arguments here. I only want to state as a fundamental principle, for which proofs can easily be offered, that memory is essential to self-identity and self-identity to the achievement of appropriate goals.

One would think that this generalization is a truism that requires no explanation or justification in the Christian Church. After all, as the Church ends its second millennium, it is one of the oldest and most enduring institutions in the world. It has, or at least should have, a long memory, a rich tradition of experience that stretches across cultural and geographical boundaries and that transcends barriers of time, class, and race.

The impression, however, that the Church often gives is of an institution that is suffering from collective amnesia. The American Protestant churches in particular, with their passion for action over thought, frequently appear to be sounding boards for causes whose connection to the Christian gospel is tenuous at best. Agendas set by secular culture, however worthy in themselves, are adopted without serious theological reflection on their place and significance in the larger Christian mission.

I do not want to be misunderstood as arguing that the Church cannot do new things in changed circumstances or that the Christian past should be allowed to lock the Church into traditional patterns of thought and action. The Christian past like the Christian present is subject to the judgment of the gospel. It is not only something to be celebrated; it is also in certain respects something to be overcome. Therefore memory has an important negative as well as positive theological function. It reminds us of mistakes to be avoided, of roads we ought not to choose, of bitter cul-de-sacs from which there is no easy or honorable exit.

The purpose of the Church is to confess by word and deed the good news of God, that God has acted in Jesus Christ to create, judge, and redeem the world. That mission may involve the Church in experimental social ministries or in political action. It will certainly require the Church to continue its traditional ministry of preaching, teaching, celebration of the sacraments, ordination of ministers, administration of the churches, and prayer.

The Christian past, both in its positive and in its negative aspects, places a question mark over Christian thinking and acting in the present. Every generation in the Church is sensitive to certain themes in the gospel, while remaining insensitive to other themes. In our attempt to understand and do the Word of God in our generation, we need therefore to listen to the voices of obedient hearers of the Word in other generations, in order to learn from them what we can no longer teach one another.

Most of the essays in this book are not, strictly speaking, historical studies. They are theological essays which attempt to apply historical insights to specific problems in the life and mission of the Church. They are, in other words, attempts to jog the memory of modern Christians, to remind us where we have been as we attempt to determine where we ought to go.

The essays on the minister as preacher and teacher were composed with the struggle of Protestant churches to come to terms with their tradition of the "learned minister" in mind. Preaching and teaching have been denigrated as functions of the ministerial office in favor of models of the minister as a catalyst for social change and action. These essays reaffirm the role of preaching and teaching as essential functions of the ordained ministry, which can be enriched by other functions but never replaced.

The essay on conversion was commissioned by

11

Theology Today, which wanted to reexamine the meaning of conversion in the evangelistic mission of the Church. I try to show that conversion in the context of Reformation theology has a somewhat different meaning from the meaning it has traditionally been assigned in American Evangelicalism and that this broader meaning has important implications for the way the Church should conceive its teaching and preaching mission, both to the outsider and to the faithful who regularly fill its pews.

The essay on Asbury was written at a time when my own communion, The United Methodist Church, was trying to redefine its understanding of the ordained ministry in relationship to lay ministries. Appeals were made to the Bible and to the present practices of the various Christian churches without attention to the specific history that had shaped the Wesleyan understanding of ministry. I have included this essay because the questions raised and the solutions proposed have importance for a wider ecumenical audience.

The essays on the status of women and on Mary were stimulated by related, but slightly different, problems. The first essay was written in response to the contention that the Reformation had worsened the lot of women by destroying the religious orders in which women had exercised independence and authority in the Church. It seems to me that the problem is a good deal more complex than conventional wisdom implies. The Protestant attack on the celibate ethic had positive implications for the status of women and even paved the way for their eventual ordination in the Christian ministry.

The second essay was written after attendance at a service in a university chapel celebrating the contribution of women to Church and society but with no reference to biblical women, least of all to the Virgin Mary. The essay, by putting forward an evangelical Mariology, is an implicit attack on the unbiblical neglect of Mary by Protestants.

The doctrine of the Trinity has been reopened for the Church by Christians who insist that the language of Father, Son, and Spirit be replaced by the more inclusive terms Creator, Redeemer, and Sustainer. Unfortunately, what seems like a simple solution to a tangled and difficult problem is really no solution at all and leaves the congregations who adopt that language wedded to ancient heresies they had no intention of reviving. If the language must be changed (and the burden of proof is still on the changers), then the language adopted must carry the theological weight borne by the earlier terms.

The essay on the superiority of pre-critical exegesis addresses a problem that the Church experiences every Sunday, when ministers, who have been taught to use historical-critical tools in biblical interpretation and never to allegorize, allegorize when they preach and very seldom use historical-critical tools. The assumption has been that the problem is with ministers, who need to repent and change their ways to match the lectures they heard in seminary. My own contention is that the problem is less with ministers than with the theory they have been taught.

The last essay in the book deals with the problem of spiritual formation. Before Christians from Reformation churches search for devotional classics and meditative techniques from other religions or from Christian traditions very different from their own, they need to examine whether there are usable resources from their own tradition for the nurture of the spiritual life. In the reformation tradition, theology and prayer are not conceived as antithetical but as coinherent. What makes a theologian, as Luther rightly argued, is meditation, temptation, and prayer.

I am grateful to Dennis Campbell and Stanley Hauerwas, who read the manuscript of this book in its earlier form and made valuable suggestions for its improvement.

I would like to dedicate these essays to my students at three institutions—Harvard Divinity School, Lancaster Theological Seminary, and Duke Divinity School—who stimulated me to write them, sometimes by the questions they asked, sometimes by the questions they answered.

Memory and Mission

ONE

The Necessity
of the Past

Americans are not as a matter of course oriented toward the past. There are any number of historical reasons why they are not. America represented for the immigrant populations of Europe an attempt to break with the Old World and to make a fresh start, untrammeled by the past. Most of the immigrants to the New World had good reasons for trying to begin again, for wanting to forget the past. Some had been persecuted for their faith, some for their politics. And those who had not been persecuted either left because they were in severe economic straits or because they believed they could improve their economic situation in a land hospitable to new beginnings and careless of the past. After all, why would anyone want to leave Europe and face the dangers and uncertainties of the American frontier, if the situation in one's native land were comfortable and secure? There were, of course, adventurers who found excitement in the harsh American frontier lands and indentured servants, especially African slaves, who were compelled to come. More frequently, the immigrant was a person who wanted to begin again and who had reason to forget the past.

I

The task of nation-building consumed energies and talents that in Europe could be devoted to culture and the arts. Art requires leisure and there was little of that on the frontier. The frontier was egalitarian. It judged people by what they could do and not by what they had been or by what services their families had rendered to society in the twelfth century. If men and women could bear their share of the weight and were honest in their dealings with their neighbors, no one was inclined to be inquisitive about their past. The talents that were valued on the frontier were useful talents, immediately useful for survival in a harsh and primitive situation. If people wanted to write novels or read history, that was their business—provided they knew how to make an immediate contribution to frontier society and did not expect others to do their work while they read and thought. Folk could live on the frontier without knowing how to read; they could not live without knowing how to hunt, fish, spin, weave, trap, farm, clear land, carpenter, shoe a horse, and defend themselves.

That does not mean that Americans lived altogether without a sense of history. They commemorated their national heroes and events.

But the past played a lesser role for them than did the future. There were no Roman ruins in Kentucky, no castles of robber barons along the Missouri River. Americans were not surrounded by memorials of the past. The great fact for American life was the frontier. Or perhaps I should put that differently; the great fact that confronted Americans on every hand was the seemingly limitless space. There were new lands to be opened up, new resources to be exploited, new possibilities for movement and migration. The future offered rugged individuals, who were willing to take risks, the possibilities of making their fortunes in a land their ancestors had never seen.

In Europe, the land had been divided centuries before; movement and migration were restricted; national boundaries were clearly known as were social and economic boundaries. A child, born in Europe, knew what the future held; it held largely what the past had held for the generations of men and women born before. The possibilities were clearly marked out and they were limited. Not so the American frontier. The future on the American frontier was a time of limitless possibilities or so at least it seemed. And not only so, but the possibilities that confronted the children were always believed to be better than the possibilities that confronted their parents and grandparents. Americans were future-oriented. The future was hopeful, fraught with new and unknown possibilities. And there was in the indeterminate and hopeful future a solution for every problem. Europeans might feel in advance that a problem

19

was insoluble, if for no other reason than that their forbears thought it was insoluble. But Americans were not burdened with such respect for the opinions of the past. They did not know that a problem was insoluble until they themselves tried to solve it and failed. Even then they were convinced that their own failure did not rule out the possibility of the later success of someone else. The future was hopeful; no one knew in advance the limits of its possibilities; and for every problem there was a solution.

The American attitude toward Europe and toward the European past has been complicated by still another fact, the belief in American innocence and boundless good will. Puritans came to America to found a Holy Commonwealth, a city that should be set on a hill as an example to the nations. Americans in every generation since have been seeking to build the kingdom of God in America. Europe represented for America not only the past, which they were eager to forget, but a corrupt past, from whose contamination they wished to escape. The ocean served as insulation against the influences of a decadent Old World. Here in America they could build the Holy Commonwealth or the Great Society (a secular version of the same thing), unhindered by the baleful influences of the past. Americans believed that God was making in their country a new beginning. Therefore for Americans the past is not so much something to be studied as it is something to be overcome.

These attitudes toward the past place the American church in an awkward position. The plain fact is that the Church cannot escape the past, however much it may wish to. It cannot escape the past because of the nature of the Christian faith that rests on an appeal to certain events in the past. Those events are claimed by the Church (and that claim has, of course, been contested) to be not only decisive for its own faith, but absolutely crucial for the history of the world. That means absolutely crucial for the history and destiny of people who have no interest at all in these events or who have never heard about them. The Apostles' Creed, recited in most Christian churches (if not every Sunday, at least occasionally), is itself evidence of this appeal to history. Consider the verbs that are used: "conceived . . . born . . . suffered . . . crucified . . . buried . . . descended . . . rose again." When Christians recite the Creed, they point to this history, to this story of Jesus of Nazareth, whom the Church claims to be the Word and Deed of God in history. The Church confesses that the salvation of the world was effected in the life, death, and resurrection of this Man. Not all Christians understand these events in the same way. But regardless of how they explain them, they all without fail appeal to them.

Of course, there are some people who are radically skeptical about knowledge of the past, especially the past that the Church confesses to be important, but also, when pressed, about the past in general. In the nineteenth century, radical historical skepticism was in great vogue. The critical intelligence of historians, for a brief period at least, ran amok. Radical skepticism eventually died a natural death. No one refuted it; indeed, no convincing arguments could be adduced to refute it. As a philosophical position it was airtight. What finally did it in was common sense. Historians found that people who began by doubting whether Caesar crossed the Rubicon ended by doubting whether their latchkeys would fit their front doors. If radical skepticism concerning the first problem did not lead them in time to radical skepticism concerning the second, it was either because they were not logically consistent or because they were cursed with a lamentably pragmatic disposition, untouched by philosophic reasoning and probably untouchable. In short, the arguments of the radical historians proved to be very much like the arguments of a madman. They were logical, flawless in their rational consistency, but they were too small to fit reality. Human life is not possible without memory, certainly not in the short run—and not in the long run either.

Memory is not the faculty that enables us to escape from a present that we find distressing or boring into a past no longer strange and therefore manageable. Even Zwingli, who liked to stress the memorial aspect of the Lord's Supper, its intractably past dimension, did so not because he thought memory was a faculty for taking us out of the present. Zwingli was too much of an Augustinian for that. Memory is a faculty that takes some aspect of the past and makes it a datum of my present, as real and tangible as the pew on which I am sitting or the neighbor who is seated beside me. Memory grasps the past and makes it a part of my present. It does so because I need that past in order to function in the present. It is for the sake of the present that memory lays hold of the events of the past.

II

Christian faith is based on certain remembered events in history, above all, on the resurrection of Jesus Christ from the dead. The resurrection is the key event on which all else depends. First Corinthians 15:14 is a text that the Church cannot circumvent: "If Christ has not been raised, then our preaching is in vain and your faith is in vain." No resurrection, no Christianity.

This means that Christianity is not first of all an appeal to philosophy. Early Gentile Christians were not terribly interested in history. They were under the influence of an outlook that tended to depreciate what happened in history and that stressed the importance of eternal and unchanging truth, a realm of ideas above history that could be penetrated by the disciplined reason of a philosopher. In explaining the Christian faith and in recommending it to their contemporaries, Gentile Christians did make use of philosophical ideas and categories so deeply ingrained in them that they could not imagine a way of looking at the world that dispensed with them entirely. But however useful Gentile Christians imagined philosophy to be, they did not lose, except perhaps momentarily, their hold on history. Greek philosophy was used by Christians to explain to themselves and to the pagan world how God had entered history in Jesus of Nazareth. There were then, as there are now, philosophical ideas on which Christians and non–Christians can agree; and philosophy has been used with varying degrees of adequacy as a means of interpreting the Christian faith. But Christian faith does not rest on any single philosophy—not on Platonism, nor on Aristotelianism, nor on Kantianism, nor on Hegelianism, nor on existentialism, nor on process thought. The Christian faith rests on past events, which it believes to be crucial.

This also means that Christianity is not an appeal to ethics. There have been attempts to locate the significance of Christianity in the ethical precepts of the teaching of Jesus, precepts that existed before he enunciated them and that are valid apart from all consideration of the events of his life. History is denigrated, not in favor of metaphysics (with its abstract arguments) but in favor of morality (with its well-scrubbed and respectable face). But to praise the moral teaching and dispense with the figure of Jesus is to turn the New Testament on its head. From the standpoint of the Christian faith, the importance of Jesus of Nazareth is not that he uttered the Golden Rule, but that he was conceived, born, suffered, crucified, died, buried, rose. This means that my faith as a Christian is inextricably bound up with those events of the past. To be a Christian is by definition to be involved in the past, if only for the sake of the present and future.

III

There is, of course, a catch. Whether we know it or not and whether we think it is a good idea or not, our understanding of the Christian faith is influenced by the Christian tradition in which we stand. We inherit more than a New Testament account of the life, death, and resurrection of Jesus Christ; we inherit a traditional understanding of it. What we sometimes naïvely assume to be a biblical idea is not directly stated in the Bible at all (at least not in the meaning we attach to it), but is either a deduction from selected data or is a probable explanation of certain muddy and ambiguous passages. Our understanding of the Christian faith, quite apart from the question of whether we find this desirable or not, has been influenced by post-biblical developments in the Christian Church.

The doctrine of the Trinity provides a familiar example of the way in which the later Church reflected on the Bible and shaped our understanding of it. We are all acquainted, more or less, with the outcome of the trinitarian controversies. It is reflected in the hymn: "God in three persons, blessed Trinity." Is the word "Trinity" a biblical term? Do we find it anywhere in the Old or New Testaments? The answer, of course, is no. What do we find in the Bible? The Greek Fathers would have said that we find in the Old Testament the confession that God is one and in the New Testament the three names, Father, Son, and Holy

Spirit. How are these three names related to the confession that God is one? The Bible does not answer that question. The doctrine of the Trinity is the answer that the early Church hammered out as it tried to reconcile its belief in the oneness of God with its conviction that God was revealed as Father, Son, and Holy Spirit. Anyone who has studied theology knows how difficult this question was to answer and how reluctantly the Church came up with its solution.

The doctrine of the Trinity is not found in the Bible, but it represents the attempt of the Church to make sense out of what it did find there. In arriving at its position the Church weighed and rejected dynamic and modalistic Monarchianism, Tritheism, and Arianism, all of which offered alternative explanations of the biblical evidence. When I read the baptismal formula in the Gospel of Matthew ("Make disciples of all nations, baptizing them in the name of the Father and of the Son and of the Holy Spirit," Matt. 28:19) and think to myself, "Aha, the doctrine of the Trinity!" I do so because my understanding of the primitive faith of the Church has been influenced and shaped by all the generations of Christian interpreters who stand between me and the apostolic age.

Church history helps us become self-conscious concerning our dependence on the traditions of the past. It thereby gives us the freedom, when necessary, to become critical of those traditions. People who believe that they have no creed except the Bible will, I am sorry to say, be victimized by the past. So too will those innocent souls who believe that the history of the world begins with the birth of their own consciousness.

Let me quickly add that I do not think that it is a bad thing for the Christian Church in the present to be influenced by the Church of the past in its understanding of the Christian faith. Quite the contrary, it is not only inevitable that the Church in the present will be influenced by the past, it is even desirable. What is intolerable in a Christian theologian or pastor is to be unaware of that influence. As long as we do not understand the role of tradition in shaping our faith and influencing our actions, we will allow it to control us unconsciously. That is not to say that this is always reprehensible and may not be turned to good use by a wise providence. We may be under the influence of traditions that lead us into a faithful apprehension of the gospel and that provide reliable guidelines for responsible action in the present. But we may also be misled and misguided by tradition. As long as we accept uncritically what we have received from the past, we put ourselves unreservedly in its power. Tradition can obscure as well as clarify the gospel. The study of Church history gives us freedom vis-à-vis the past, freedom to appropriate the wisdom of the Church's past wisdom, when we can, and to overcome its faithlessness and sin, when we must. The aim of Church history as a theological discipline is to provide the Church with a more universal and self-critical perspective within which to make responsible theological and pastoral decisions in the present. The study of Church history ought to

27

be a liberating experience as the Christian learns, in the phrase of Adolf von Harnack, "to overcome history with history," always bearing in mind that unexamined history operates as fate.

IV

Church history has an indispensable role to play as a theological stimulus and corrective. In freeing us from theological parochialism, it also results in a loss of innocence. We see how the tradition that we learned in our parish evolved over the course of the centuries and discover, sometimes to our chagrin, that our tradition, whatever else it may be, is not simply a repristination in the twentieth century of the primitive apostolic faith. As we become acquainted with traditions other than our own, we are painfully disabused of the idea that tradition A (our own) is the only possible option that the Church has followed or, indeed, can follow. When we place tradition A alongside traditions B, C, and D, we realize for the first time what tradition A really is. Through the study of Church history we become aware of the diversity of traditions in the Christian Church and we become self-critical of our own tradition. The very existence of other traditions, all claiming to be faithful to the gospel (and each with some undeniable right to do so), puts our own tradition in question. If at the end of this self-criticism we once again affirm, albeit in a modified form, tradition A, we do so because we have tested it in the light of divergent and often conflicting interpretations that challenge our own

28

point of view. This loss of innocence is absolutely essential to responsible theological work.

It is not the task of Church history to reformulate the Christian faith anew for this generation or to prescribe policies for the Church's action in the present. But by interpreting what the Church did in the past, by clarifying what the Church believed, it provides us with a more universal perspective within which to clarify our own faith and to formulate our own actions in the present. The first task of Church history as a theological discipline is to free us from our own parochialism and make us truly catholic.

The study of Church history also teaches us to make modest claims for our theology. There is a sense in which theology is a humble science. It is human reflection about divine revelation. No one can, by taking thought, initiate divine revelation nor is there any way to bypass it. Even theologians who are keen on constructing a natural theology only do so because they believe that God has previously been revealed in nature and is therefore prehensible to human reason and imagination. The Christian Church has claimed from the beginning that there is no knowledge of God apart from revelation. Theology waits humbly, hat in hand, for that revelation.

Perhaps that is not the best image. Christian theologians are not waiting for divine self-revelation, because they believe it has occurred already. Revelation is the presupposition and precondition of theology. Theology begins with a given: unless revelation, no authentically Christian theology is possible. Theology is a human enterprise. God is revealed in nature and history, and theology is reflection in time about that revelation. All theological decisions are historically conditioned; that is to say, they are the decisions of people who live and think in the categories of their own time. Christians do not simply borrow their philosophical categories from pagans in order to make their faith intelligible. They are converted along with the categories, which are embedded in their own existence. These categories partly obscure and partly clarify the revelation of God with which they deal.

Church history reminds us that all Christian doctrine, including the theologies of hope, revolution, the future, play, and the city, is historical. The norm for Christian theology is not logical consistency but faithfulness to its origin: God's revelation in time and under the conditions of finitude. Church history forces us to admit that our reflection about that revelation is inevitably a human enterprise and therefore only partly true. It is not simply the weight of the past from which the study of Church history frees us, but also from the weight of an undue and inauthentic attachment to the present.

In part we study the history of the Church in order to find answers to the questions that perplex us. But in the process of finding answers to our questions, we are opened up to new problems and learn questions that had never occurred to us before. That means that though we study the past

for the sake of the present, we proceed methodologically as though we were studying the past for
the sake of the past alone. Our questions drive us to
the sources in the first place, but if we hope to learn
from those sources then we must discover the
questions that they were originally written to
answer. Only arduous labor, an active application
of the historical imagination to the writings of the
past, will teach us what we hope to learn. It is not
true that the documents of the past speak to us
without any involvement on our part. The past is
mute until it is cross-examined. A merely passive
reading of an old theological text will teach us very
little. We must learn to ask it the kind of questions
that will spark it into life. If we ask it wrong or
foolish questions, we will be given misleading or
foolish answers.

It is both necessary and dangerous to ask our
questions of the past. If we search the past with our
questions uppermost in our minds, but do not
trouble to learn the context in which those
questions were raised in earlier centuries, we will,
to be sure, find some light on our questions. But we
will misunderstand much of what we read, and
unnecessarily and prematurely limit what we can
learn from the wisdom of the past. If, however, we
learn to come to the past on its terms and not on
ours, and if we learn to ask the questions the
documents were written to answer, we will find
more than answers to our questions. We will find
ourselves in turn questioned by our sources.
Through strange and unfamiliar debates of the
past, on the pages of ancient commentaries, in

dusty and unread books, we will suddenly find ourselves engaged by the insights of men and women long forgotten or at best dimly remembered. In a flash, our questions will be transformed by theirs. Over the bridge of the past we will enter a newer and richer world.

Historians, unlike systematic theologians, are left with historical materials that will not conform to their finer theological instincts and with results that force them to conclusions that they find personally disagreeable. There is one commandment and one only that Church historians must scrupulously observe: honor thy father and thy mother. They must accept the past as it offers itself to them. They have no god-like prerogative to bowdlerize and "improve" history. It may be true that we understand the arguments between disputants in the past better than they themselves did, but we labor under handicaps that they did not have. Luther and Eck may have lacked irenical dispositions, but they shared the same language, the same undivided Church, similar education and cultural opportunities, were acquainted personally, and must assuredly have had friends in common. With all that in their favor, they still disagreed, not once but repeatedly. I may applaud that disagreement or bemoan it; I may understand it or explain it away; but one thing I cannot do: I cannot alter it. The historical event is beyond the reach of the historian at the level of its sheer givenness.

We study the past for the sake of the present and the future, though we proceed methodologically as if the present were not our real concern. We study the past because it is able to instruct us, if we learn to ask it the right questions and discover how to engage it on its own terms. It opens us to insights, ideas, and questions we would have encountered in no other way.

V

I once attended a party where I was called on to introduce all the guests. I knew everyone there, so that was not an unreasonable request. I went around the circle of guests easily calling off the names. Then I noticed from the corner of my eye a young woman sitting on a window ledge. Suddenly I panicked. I could not remember her name. There were five guests to go. Four, three, two, and at last in shame and confusion, I had to ask her to introduce herself. My lapse of memory meant that I could no longer function effectively in the present.

I thought at the time what an awful thing it must be to lose one's memory completely. People who have lost their memories can no longer remember who they are. That means that they can no longer function effectively in the present and that they have no secure plans for the future. They have lost their past and that has emptied their present of meaning and clouded their future. We must have contact with the past, if only for the sake of the present and the future.

The Church could, I suppose, lose its memory as well. It is certainly tempted to do that often enough. But a Church that has lost its memory of the past can only wander about aimlessly in the present and despair of its future. The Church needs the past, if only for the sake of the present and the future.

The invitation to study the history of the Church is not an irrelevant call to forsake the mission of the Church and to lose oneself in a past no longer recoverable. It is rather a call to abandon peripheral matters, to put an end to aimless meanderings and nervous activism, to learn once again who we are and to whom we belong. Only when we have regained our identity from the past can we undertake our mission in the present.

TWO

Reformation and Conversion

The Reformation began, almost accidentally, as a debate over the meaning of the word "penitence." I say "accidentally" because the controversy over indulgences that set in motion the first stirrings of the Protestant Reformation seemed at the time far too limited and restrictive an issue on which to hang an entire program for the reform of the Church. Only the year before in 1516 Luther had composed a probing series of propositions on the hopeless condition of the human will without grace. He had followed it up in 1517 with a stinging barrage of ninety-seven theses against scholastic theology, theses that questioned with inescapable directness the Church's use of the philosophy of Aristotle. But when the reform began, it was not Luther's attack on the method and conclusions of German academic theology, but his criticism of the medieval theory of penance that captured the imagination of Europe.

Luther may only have intended to attack the

extravagant claims that were being advanced by the Dominican, John Tetzel, who was selling indulgences across the river in the part of Saxony under the jurisdiction of Duke George. But when Luther sat down at his desk to draw up his theses for debate, he found that he could not direct his criticisms against the narrower issue of indulgences without discussing the far broader question of the meaning of penitence.

The first thesis touches the central issue. Jesus Christ announced the imminent coming of the kingdom of God and invited his listeners to repent. What exactly, Luther asked, did he have in mind? Did he mean to urge submission to the sacrament of penance? The Latin text of the New Testament with its translation of the words of Jesus as *penitentiam agite* ("do penance") certainly could give that impression. Underneath the Latin formula of the Vulgate, however, was the original Greek verb with its Hebrew antecedents. What was demanded by the preaching of Jesus was a "conversion," a "return," a "change of mind or intention," a fundamental turning of one's life to God, which begins but does not end with the first assent of the will to the gospel.

Debate over the meaning of repentance is basic to Protestantism. From the early and formative decades of the Protestant Reformation through the evangelical awakening of the eighteenth century to the Bangkok Assembly in 1973 and the Lausanne Covenant of 1974, Protestants have returned again and again to the theme of penitence and conversion.

American Protestants are, of course, familiar with the tradition of the Evangelical Awakening, which has left its mark on American churches from the time of Edwards and Asbury to the present. Less well known, but no less important, are the reflections of the Protestant Reformers on the subject of repentance. While John Cotton was accustomed to "sweeten his mouth" with a passage from John Calvin before retiring, most American Christians are more familiar with Calvinism than with Calvin. American evangelism has been molded more by Edwards, Finney, Moody, Sunday, and Graham than by the theology of the sixteenth-century reformers.

I

Common to almost all early Protestant discussions of repentance is a barely disguised hostility to every theory of conversion that stresses proper preparation for the reception of grace. Opposition to the notion of preparation for grace led Protestants inevitably to reject all medieval theologies of penance, the most Augustinian and restrained as well as the most Pelagian and careless. Nevertheless, it is fair to state that the form in which Luther first encountered a theory of preparation for grace was the form in which it was elaborated by Gabriel Biel in his *Collectorium* on the Sentences of Peter Lombard.

Biel was the first professor of theology at the University of Tübingen, a university founded in the last quarter of the fifteenth century. Biel was balanced, judicious, immensely learned, and deeply spiritual. He was famous not only inside Germany but outside it as well; his works appeared in French as well as in German editions. But his understanding of repentance, about which he wrote learnedly and at great length, was fundamentally defective from Luther's point of view.

It was not that Biel failed to ground his arguments in the Bible or in the Augustinian tradition of the Western church. Indeed, Biel's ruminations on penitence are laced with frequent quotations from the Bible: James 4:8; Luke 11:9; Jeremiah 29:13; and above all, Zechariah 1:3: "Turn to me, says the Lord of Hosts, and I will turn unto you." The text from Zechariah summed up in the briefest possible scope the essence of Biel's theology of penance.

God has established a covenant, the terms of which are proclaimed by the Church in the gospel. God has promised to give saving grace to everyone who meets the conditions of that covenant. What is demanded of the sinner, quite simply, is that the sinner love God above everything else. Sinners can do this because, while sin has damaged their capacity for loving God, it has not obliterated it. To put it in its crassest form, grace is a reward for exemplary moral virtue, a virtue that Biel, like Kant, thought lay in the power of the unconverted will.

Luther rejected categorically this understanding of preparation for grace. Morally good acts do not have a claim on the favor of God. The real preparation for grace, if one can use this language

38

at all without occasioning misunderstanding, is the preparation that God has made by his election, calling, and gifts. Luther agreed with Biel that God has established a covenant, but it is a covenant whose basis is diametrically opposed to the covenant recommended by Biel.

God promises to give his grace to "real sinners." "Real sinners" are people who are not merely sinners in fact (everyone, after all, is a sinner in that sense), but who confess that they are sinners. "Real sinners" conform their judgment of themselves to the judgment of God over them and by doing so justify God in his Word of judgment and grace. Paradoxically, it is the "real sinner" who is justified by God and who knows both theoretically and experientially what repentance offers and demands. The gospel as Luther conceived it is both easier and harder than the gospel that Biel offered. Being a real sinner is a condition that, on the face of it, anyone can meet; but it is harder because it demands rigorous honesty in the face of the truth. Penitents cannot prepare themselves for grace because they must be crucified by the Word of God's judgment and die. Repentance has to do with death and life and not merely with the resolute decision of an already good person like Biel to improve his frankly unimpeachable character.

Luther's objection to Biel's theory is not merely that it harbors a thoroughly unrealistic view of human nature, though that is part of his objection. Even more important for Luther than the fact that no one can live up to Biel's theory of repentance is the fact that no one is expected to. The gospel does not demand moral virtue as the preparatory stage of conversion. Biel's view of the matter is not only unworkable; it is irrelevant. The sole precondition for authentic conversion is real sin; the sole preparation that matters is the preparation that God has made in the gospel.

The saying of Jesus that the whole have no need of a physician is a saying that the Church has always had great difficulty in assimilating. It seems so much more reasonable to believe that God will be merciful to those people who meet certain prior expectations: the right ideology, the right sex or race, the right degree of devotion to the causes currently supported by the right elements in society. "But when we were right," Luther observed in one of his earliest writings, "God laughed at us in our rightness."[1] God's quarrel is with the whole human race and not merely with certain factions in it. Judgment falls not only on the theologically heterodox but also on the theologically pure. The one absolutely indispensable precondition for the reception of grace is not to be right—not even in the sense of theological orthodoxy—but to be sick. The gospel is for real sinners.

II

The Church provides the context within which authentic repentance can take place. It may seem surprising to lay so much stress on the Church in early Protestant thought, since Protestants have often been regarded as religious individualists who affirmed the right of private judgment against the corporate power of the late medieval Church. But in point of fact the late medieval Church was the home of a private and individualistic piety, while Protestantism has been hopelessly social from the beginning. Whether talking of ordination or of eucharistic theory, Protestants have focused on the congregation rather than the individual as the fundamental reality from which theological reflection must proceed. Critics may accuse Protestants of talking about the Church too much or of talking about it in the wrong way, but not of neglecting it.

The Church can, of course, stand in the way of authentic conversion and in his *Reply to Sadoleto,* Calvin accused the late medieval Church of doing precisely that. In a lengthy bill of particulars Calvin charged the late medieval Church with keeping people from repentance by the disunity of its life and the disorder of its teaching. In particular the Church had urged upon the faithful a duty of implicit faith in its own teaching authority, while, to use Calvin's vivid language, the "leaders of faith neither understood [the] Word nor greatly cared for it" but taught "doctrines sprung from the human brain." Not surprisingly this "supine state of the pastors" led swiftly to the "stupidity of the people" who thought that the "highest veneration paid to [the] Word was to revere it at a distance, as a thing inaccessible, and abstain from all investigation of it."[2] Reverence for the Church—any church—in its unreformed state can only impede progress toward the radical change of direction that is demanded by Jesus in the Gospels.

Even in the worst of times the Church is, to use

41

Calvin's favorite imagery, a mother and school, which nurtures and instructs men and women in the Christian faith. When confronted by the quotation from Augustine, "I would not have believed the gospel if the authority of the Church had not moved me," Calvin agreed with it, much to the surprise of his conservative critics. The important thing, however, is not to quote Augustine—anyone armed with the *Milleloquium* can do that—but to know what he meant.

It is obvious what he did not mean. Augustine did not intend to teach that the authority of the Church is so great, so metaphysically higher in the scale of being, that the gospel derives its authority in a secondary fashion from the prior and more encompassing authority of the Church. Augustine said that he would not have believed the gospel if the authority of the Church had not moved him; he did not say, or mean to imply, that he would not have believed the gospel if a committee of bishops had not approved it. The authority of the gospel is primary and the authority of the Church is secondary and derivative.

The authority of the Church to which Augustine alluded is the authority of the holiness of its life and the faithfulness of its witness. In a word, Augustine was moved to trust the gospel because he first trusted the people who told him about it. The gospel is better than the Church, but it is never found except in the human and therefore touching witness of the Church. The Church, like the Samaritan woman, tugs at the sleeve of the unbeliever and says: "Come, see a man, which told me all the things which ever I did: is not this the Christ?" That is the authority of the Church, the authority of a faithful and self-effacing witness.

To this Church has been committed the power of the keys, the power to bind and loose the penitent from their sins. Yet it is a power that the Church does and does not have. It does not have it in the sense that it is not a power that inheres in the community as a group, as color, weight, texture are qualities of an object. But it does have it in the sense that as a community it proclaims by word and deed the authority of the gospel. The gospel binds and looses from sins, not the Church, and yet it does not do so apart from the Church that bears it and bears witness to it.

Repentance—at least repentance in the sense in which it is recommended in the New Testament—is not a spontaneous religious emotion that springs up in the human heart without prior sufficient cause. It is a response to the message of God's judgment and grace, a message proclaimed by the Church, the community established by God in which faith is formed. While the gospel can and does reach outside the Church and while God is never limited in achieving his purposes to any instrumental means, nevertheless, the Church is the principal sphere and context for authentic conversion. Repentance is, if you will not misunderstand me, a churchly function. Indeed, it is the perpetual activity of a Church reformed by the Word of God.

III

The repentance to which a Christian is called is a continuous and lifelong process. While conversion

43

begins, as everything in history does, at some point in time, the process of conversion is not completed until every aspect of the human personality is driven out into the light of God's severe mercy, judged and renewed. Conversion proceeds layer by layer, relationship by relationship, here a little, there a little, until the whole personality and not merely one side of it has been recreated by God. Conversion refers not only to the initial moment of faith, no matter how dramatic or revolutionary it may seem, but to the whole life of the believer and the network of relationships in which that life is entangled: personal, familial, social, economic, political.

That is why the Church is called a school. Faith is not only something we have; it is something we are learning. Mastery of the Greek alphabet is not the same thing as mastery of the "Odyssey"; yet mastery of the one proceeds from mastery of the other. The first moment of penitence initiates one into the school of faith, but the lessons to be learned can only be grasped by long and patient experience. Conversion, to change the metaphor, is not only the little wicket gate through which John Bunyan's pilgrim quickly passes as he abandons the City of Destruction; it is the entire pilgrimage to the Celestial City.

No aspect of Reformation teaching on penitence is more foreign to the American evangelical experience of the past two centuries than the stress on conversion as a process rather than as a crisis in human life. Evangelicals have always emphasized the initial moment of faith in which one passes from death to life, from darkness to light. This is a moment celebrated, recalled, and, when the experience fades, recaptured. While sanctification may be a process, conversion is the work of a moment.

The Protestant reformers did not agree, but that was not because they despised the first stirrings of faith or the resolute convictions of people who bore witness to what they had seen and heard. They did not agree because they had a somewhat different doctrine of sin and were convinced that sin was such a complex phenomenon and so intricately embedded in human thinking and willing that only a thousand conversions would root it out.

Or maybe I have put that too negatively. The Reformers were convinced that only those who love God can hate sin. A thoroughly unconverted sinner is a perfect child in his knowledge of sin. Only a saint knows what sin is and therefore only a person who has progressed in the love of God can see with sufficient clarity what exactly is the character of the sin that is distorting his life. It requires some growth in grace to repent properly. The more one grows in the love of God, the more perfect one's repentance. Mourners sitting on the anxious bench or filing into an inquirer's room have, unfortunately, only a child's eye view of their own sin. Real repentance, real conversion of life, is an activity of the spiritually mature.

Repentance is consistently portrayed by the Reformers as a return to baptism, a return to the foundation of God's gifts and promises, which are generous enough to sustain us throughout our

whole life. They must be reappropriated, reaf-
firmed; they cannot be superseded. By the process
of repentance, of continuous conversion, we
appropriate the mercy and gifts of God at a deeper
level than we have ever experienced them before.

Perhaps the most striking image of baptism in
early Protestant literature is the one offered by
Huldrych Zwingli. Baptism is like the cowl or
uniform that is given to a novice in a mendicant
order. The young boy of twelve is a Franciscan or a
Dominican from the very moment he accepts the
uniform and the obligations that wearing it entails.
But he is not a Franciscan in the same sense as an
old brother of eighty-two, who has worn the brown
robe of St. Francis all his long and varied life. The
young novice must grow up into the uniform he
has been given. So, too, baptism is our uniform; we
must grow up into it. It is cut for a far more
generously proportioned figure than ours. But we
will grow up into it as we are continuously
converted at ever deeper levels of our personality
by means of the Word of God. Conversion does not
bypass baptism; it fits us to it, so that we take all that
is offered and become all we profess.

IV

Every conversion has a price. Something is
gained, but something is lost as well and the loss
may prove to be painful. There is a tendency in
certain circles of American evangelicalism to offer
the gospel as the solution for pressing human
problems without mentioning that there is another

side to the question. The gospel not only resolves problems that trouble us; it creates problems that we never had before and that we would gladly avoid.

Sometimes the problems are vocational. In his Preface to the *Commentary on the Psalms,* published in 1557, Calvin, who was generally reluctant to offer any information about himself in his published works, broke his silence to talk about his sudden and unexpected conversion to Protestantism. In a brief passage of unusual candor Calvin confessed that his principal ambition both before and after his conversion was to lead the quiet life of a humanist scholar, alone with his books, his commentaries, and his grammars. Against his own personal preferences he was driven by God to assume a role in shaping history.

Sometimes life itself is at stake. It makes sober reading to examine the pages of the *Martyr's Mirror* and to realize that almost none of the first generation of leaders of the Anabaptist moment lived to see that movement reach its tenth anniversary. Not all the martyrs were Anabaptist; certainly not all were Protestant. From William Tyndale to Edmund Campion, from Robert Barnes to Thomas More, from Hugh Latimer to John Fisher, conversion to Christ in the sixteenth century could entail the loss of one's own life. The age could, and frequently did, exact a grisly price for heeding the radical call of Jesus to turn about in one's tracks and head in a diametrically opposite direction.

Yet most frequently the problems are what one

might loosely call moral problems. Every human decision has its moral aspects and since every human decision is qualified by obedience to the demand of the gospel for repentance and conversion, human life is somewhat more complicated than it was before. It is no longer possible simply to adopt the customary attitudes toward war or race or business or marriage or abortion or any other question that affects individual or corporate life. Every decision stands under the question posed by the words of Jesus: "Repent, for the kingdom of God is at hand!"

Calvin describes the life of the converted by two ponderous phrases: mortification of the flesh and vivification of the Spirit. The first phrase is clear enough; it means death to the old way of thinking and acting. But the second phrase is the one not to be lost sight of. The death of the old is for the sake of the birth of a new reality.

Luther was fond of talking about the strange and proper work of God. The strange work of God refers to the work of wrath and judgment; the proper work designates the work of mercy and renewal. Both were spoken of in the Bible but they were not given equal emphasis. Their relationship is dialectical. God does the strange work of judgment and destruction for the sake of the proper work of mercy and love. The old, unrepentant, faithless, unconverted reality must be destroyed, but not as an end in itself. God destroys the old decadent self in order to create in its place a new reality almost too glorious to be imagined. Suffering is for the sake of joy.

48

V

These four themes from early Protestant thought—the denial of the possibility of preparation for the reception of grace, the insistence on the Church as the context in which genuine repentance takes place, the description of conversion as a continuous and lifelong process, and the warning that there is no conversion that does not exact a price from the penitent—are certainly not the only themes that need to be considered by the Church in the present as it ponders its own evangelistic mission. Indeed, they may even need to be corrected by insights derived from the Bible or other voices in the Christian tradition. But they are insights that cannot be lightly set aside. As Calvin observed, when we deal with repentance and the forgiveness of sins, we are dealing with "the sum of the gospel."[3]

NOTES

1. *D. Martin Luthers Werke: Kritische Gesamtausgabe* (Weimar, 1883), 56.449.1-6.
2. John C. Olin, ed., *John Calvin and Jacopo Sadoleto: A Reformation Debate* (New York: Harper & Row, 1966), p. 82.
3. *Institutes* III.iii.1.

THREE

"Woe to me if I do not preach the Gospel!"

That strikes most of us, if we are honest with ourselves, as an exaggerated sentiment. It is difficult from our own experience of listening to sermons in Protestant parishes to understand the sense of passionate urgency that prompted this confession from Paul. A sense of urgency is not the feeling most commonly inspired by Protestant preaching. There is little said in the average sermon that could not just as well be put off until next Sunday or the Sunday after that. It is, I am afraid, an infrequent experience for Protestant worshipers to leave morning worship with a stunned sense of having been confronted with the inescapable issues of life and death. Preaching, which in the words of the late B. L. Manning was meant to be a "manifestation of the incarnate Word from the written word by the spoken word," has become in our day a bland repetition of religious platitudes and folk wisdom—familiar, predictable, and boring. Small wonder that many critics of the

Church have suggested that preaching will in the future be at best a minor function of the ordained ministry.

Preaching has not always been held in such low repute by Protestants. Indeed, it was the central act of Puritan worship. To say that preaching was well regarded by the Puritans is to raise as many problems as it solves. One of the most difficult things about Puritanism is to say exactly what it was. It has been used, of course, as an unflattering epithet to describe a Christian piety gone sour, an unlovely legalism more interested in enforcing a series of rules than in commending the love of God. And yet if there is anything characteristic of Puritanism, it is the intensity and depth of its religious experience. Puritanism is an experiential or "experimental" religion and the Puritan is a person who claims to have had a living experience of the God of wrath and redemptive love, however set and logical the formulae may be that he uses to describe this experience. John Bunyan claimed to preach "what I felt, what I smartingly did feel."

The Puritans, without entertaining any illusion about the limitations of the candidates ordained to preach in their churches, still regarded the pulpit as the throne of God and the sermon as the principal means for the extension of the rule of God over creation. The Puritan divine, therefore, was under heavy obligation to be prepared before he preached and a welcome compliment was to say that the "sermon was well-studied." For the Puritans the text of Paul, "Woe to me if I do not preach the gospel," was not difficult to understand.

51

The King's business was transacted in a preeminent way by the proclamation of the gospel from the pulpit. To stand in the pulpit was to stand on the barricades of the kingdom of God. Nothing could be more relevant, nothing more decisive for human destiny.

Of course, even then the sermon was under attack as an ineffective or secondary means for furthering the work of the Church in the world. There have been, and still are, four fundamental objections to preaching as an activity of the Church. These objections may be imperfectly summarized as sacramentalism, spiritualism, rationalism, and activism. Let us look briefly at each in turn.

1. *Sacramentalism.* The medieval understanding of preaching regards the sermon as preparation for the reception of grace through the sacraments. The sermon calls the congregation to the sacraments. The medieval image is the image of a priest, standing on the steps of the cathedral, calling men and women to come inside to the confessional, the baptismal font, or the altar rail. God does not give grace through the sermon or, at best, he gives a kind of preparatory grace. But the action of God in forgiving sins takes place in the sacraments.

This attitude toward preaching is well illustrated by a conversation that took place between Reinhold and Ursula Niebuhr and that Reinhold Niebuhr reports in his essay, "Sunday Morning Debate."

My wife and I were on our way to the Sunday morning service at the cathedral. To compensate her for the number of times she has to hear me preach I go with her on my two free Sundays of the year to the cathedral. This bargain is further weighted to my advantage by the graceful concession from my wife which permits such tardy arrival that we can miss the sermon and yet hear the litany. "We Anglicans," declared my wife, "do not need a sermon if we have the service. There is more genuine religion in a well-sung litany than in any sermon." I agreed to that. A good boys' choir covers a multitude of sermons, particularly if the sexless and austere beauty of its song echoes through the majestic vaults of a cathedral. It is too bad that there are so few places where you can hear both a vigorous sermon and a good choir.

My spouse countered this by enumerating the parsons in her denomination whom I like to hear preach. There are quite a number, I admit. "You may have more good preachers than we," she said, "but you need them more desperately and do not have them in proportion to your need. We do not need them."

The Protestant understanding is that preaching is an action. If you like, it is a sacramental act. In and through the words of the preacher, the Word of God confers grace, works the forgiveness of sins, awakes and nurtures faith. In the Catholic sacraments something is both symbolized and brought about. In Protestant preaching, when it is a preaching of the Word of God, something is both symbolized and brought about. The role played by sacraments in Roman Catholic thought is taken over in Protestant thought by the preaching of the Word of God. Even baptism and the Lord's Supper are for Protestants only a visible Word, a visible preaching. It is not water that cleanses from sin but the promise of God attached to the water, which must be apprehended in faith.

Under the impact of Protestant thought, Roman Catholic theology has developed a similar theology of the preached word. And yet I cannot help but feel when I read contemporary Catholic theologians that the renewed emphasis on preaching as a kind of sacramental action is still thought of within a medieval framework. For a Protestant it is through preaching that God forgives sins. For a Catholic, preaching, though an act of God that confers grace, confers really a kind of preparatory grace, that must be consummated in the sacraments to be effective. Sin is still forgiven in the confessional booth. I have yet to read a Roman Catholic author who abandons this understanding, however much he may wish to stress the importance of preaching and of a theology of the Word of God. But I could be mistaken.

2. *Spiritualism.* A second objection is the one raised by the spiritualists. Spiritualists, in the sense in which I am using the word, are not people who believe in ESP and who attempt to contact late Aunt Minnie who succumbed to pneumonia last winter. They are people who believe that religion is essentially a private matter, that inner spirituality is more important than the performance of ritual acts, and that the test of authentic piety is its ability to motivate people to achieve concrete ethical goals.

Perhaps the clearest statement of the spiritualist objection to preaching can be found in the debate that took place in the sixteenth century between Martin Luther and an itinerant school teacher from Nuremberg, Hans Denck. Both Luther and Denck agreed that God can only be known through his self-revelation in the Word. But here the agreement ends and the differences begin to multiply. Preaching is not an essential activity for Denck because God speaks directly to the human heart. God's Word is not an esoteric or fantastic religious experience. It is the voice of the Logos who calls men and women to obedience to God. While there are millions of people who have not read the Bible and who cannot hear the proclamation of the gospel, there is no person who has not heard the inner voice of God. Because the Word of God speaks to all men and women, all people are responsible to God and cannot plead that they have never heard the message of redemption or were not predestined to receive grace. Human beings do not initiate their own salvation, but they are free to accept or reject the claim of God laid immediately upon them by the divine Word. Spiritualism is a religion of the inner Word.

For Luther, however, and for Protestantism generally, the Word of God is something external before it is something internal. It is not the case that the Word of God speaks directly to the human heart without external mediation. The Word of God is something spoken, written, and preached—all external acts. God has made himself known in the concrete humanity of Jesus Christ. He has bound his Spirit to the apostolic testimony of Holy Scripture. God comes to human beings from without, through the elements of bread and wine or through the proclamation of the gospel. Faith is not something that by a kind of spontaneous generation sprouts up suddenly in the human heart. It is an answer to a Word spoken to it from without.

The spiritualists, by beginning with what they believe to be the still, small voice of God spoken in secret to their heart, make it impossible to distinguish the voice of God from the voice of their own imagination. But even more dangerously, they unwittingly provide sinners with an excuse for their disobedience to God. If revelation is an inner voice, then God is bound to the sensitivity of human religious intuition. Those who have no religious experiences cannot be held accountable for their rebellion against God. For Luther it is precisely the fact that the Word of God is not dependent upon human receptivity that it can effectively unmask human pretension and sin. God's Word has universal validity apart from human experience and even, perhaps, in spite of it.

3. *Rationalism.* The third objection to preaching is closely related to the second. It is a small and almost imperceptible step from the inner voice of spiritual experience to the inner voice of reason. Preaching is unnecessary for the rationalist because it only tells him what he knows already if he listens to the voice of common sense, if he follows the moral instinct that is the inalienable possession of every rational person.

When I was a graduate student at Harvard, I used to pass a museum of German art on my way to the divinity school. On the front and sides of this museum were carved in stone several famous quotations from German literature. I remember in particular the quotation carved over the side door. I assumed it was from Kant though it was unidentified. The quotation read as follows: *Du kannst denn du sollst.* Freely translated it means: you can do it because you should do it. Your abilities correspond to your duties; your duties are not heavier than your abilities can bear. That is all you know and all you need to know. It is the sum and substance of true religion. You can do it because you should do it.

In the eighteenth century a great many people thought of Christianity as a series of duties, known to all men and women of good will apart from revelation. When John Toland called his famous treatise, *Christianity Not Mysterious,* he made clear by that title the general disposition of his time. For Toland and those who shared his views, Christianity was a rational, natural religion. What is mysterious, Toland felt, is irrelevant and really not worth consideration by rational people. Particular religions are important only insofar as they embody ideas and moral standards common to the human race. True religion is natural religion. It is the religion held everywhere by all people at all times. Christianity and Buddhism are not important in themselves; they are important only insofar as they each, in their own way, witness to a common natural religion. What is distinctive about a religion is by the same token false. Christianity is morality and Jesus is important as a moral teacher.

Benjamin Franklin summarized very well the basic presuppositions of people who felt this way when he wrote in his autobiography: "I never doubted the existence of the Deity, that he made the world, and governed it by his Providence; that the most acceptable service of God was the doing good to man; that our souls are immortal; and that all crime will be punished, and virtue rewarded, either here or hereafter." In short, for Benjamin Franklin as for Toland and Kant, the essence of Christianity is morality.

This approach to Christianity tended to undermine the importance and centrality of Jesus Christ. The moral law, the duty that God requires, is written on the human heart. We do not learn the moral law from Christ. We know it already. We only see illustrated in the life of Christ something that we know independently of him. When Jesus uttered his moral teaching, he was pointing out great truths which were known before Jesus uttered them and which are valid even if Jesus had never taught them. Christianity, these people argued, is reducible to morality. While Jesus fulfilled a useful role as a moral teacher and example, he is not necessary to Christianity. The moral law, which is the only really important thing, can be known apart from Jesus and thus apart from the preaching of the Church.

Nor is this approach to Christianity wholly out of fashion. When Dr. James Luther Adams of Harvard Divinity School was riding on a train from New York to Boston, he happened to sit down beside an astronomer. The two men struck up a conversation about theology and for the better part of the trip across the Connecticut countryside they discussed the meaning of the Christian faith. Finally, as the train pulled into the station in Boston the astronomer, reaching for his hat and coat, said, "Come now, Dr. Adams, isn't it true that the whole of Christianity can be summed up in the Golden Rule?"

"Of course," snapped Dr. Adams, "and all astronomy can be summed up as 'twinkle, twinkle, little star.' "

Rationalism draws a circle too small to contain reality and the rationalist objection to preaching ends by reducing Jesus Christ to an addendum, a footnote to a system that is complete without him.

4. *Activism.* The final objection to preaching is the objection of the activist, who regards talk as ambiguous and who considers the language of deeds to be the only valid speech. Talk is cheap; works of love are what count. The Church needs to do less talking and more acting. It must become involved in human suffering along the Jericho roads of this world.

While this strikes us as a peculiarly modern objection to preaching, it, too, has a long history. Perhaps the most famous critic of the Church that talks but does not act is Thomas Muentzer, who perished in the Peasant's Revolt of 1525. Muentzer attacked all Christendom, but especially Martin Luther, who according to Muentzer had made Christianity too easy by preaching a honey-sweet Christ. Muentzer called him Dr. Lügner, Dr. Liar. Luther, he said, only asks people to believe, which is an easy thing to do, and neglects the really difficult part of the gospel, which is living a life of obedient discipleship.

Luther replied that Muentzer had turned the gospel on its head. Faith is the real problem, not works. Anyone can show kindness to a neighbor, but to risk one's life on what appear to be the insubstantial promises of God is not a simple matter. Faith is not merely assent to propositions. It is the committal of the whole self to God without visible guarantees that such commitment is a sane and sensible thing to do. Life is at risk in faith and not merely religious opinions.

None of these objections finally satisfies us. We cannot play preaching off against the Lord's Supper, since preaching is itself a sacramental act. We cannot escape from the proclamation of the Church to our inner experience without entering a dream world in which it is impossible to distinguish the authentic voice of God from the projections of our own fantasies and desires. We cannot flee to the rationalism of Kant and Franklin without embracing a religion that does not find a necessary place for Jesus Christ. We cannot lose ourselves in doing without facing the nagging doubt that the really difficult question is the question of being. It is, after all, entirely possible that the words, "thou fool, this night thy soul shall be required of thee," could be spoken to a minister or social worker as well as to a businessman. Babbitt is not the only one who stands in peril of soul.

Perhaps we have analyzed the crisis of our age incorrectly. Perhaps Paul's confession, "Woe to me if I do not preach the gospel!" is normative and our tongue-tied hesitancy aberrational rather than the other way around. Perhaps, just perhaps, it is not preaching that is at fault, but our preaching.

Luther drew a distinction between two kinds of words in order to make clear what the Bible means when it speaks of the Word of God. There is, of course, the *Heissel-Wort*, the Call-Word, the word that we use when we apply names to things that already exist. The biblical story of Adam in the garden is a fine example of this. He names all the creatures. He does not create them; he only sorts them out and gives them labels.

But a second kind of word, the *Thettel-Wort* or Deed-Word, not only names but effects what it says. Adam looks around him and says, "There is a cow and an owl and a horse and a mosquito." But God looks around him and says, "Let there be light," and there is light.

God's Word is a Deed-Word; it creates new possibilities where no possibilities existed before. The Word of God is a Word that enriches the poor, releases the captives, gives sight to the blind, and sets at liberty those who are oppressed.

The Word that the Church proclaims is a Deed-Word. It is a Word that meets human beings at the point of their greatest need and liberates them. The Church that has become modest about the proclamation of the gospel is not a Church that has become more relevant to the human situation, but less so.

During World War II a courier service was developed from occupied Norway to neutral

Sweden. Bishop Odd Hagen of Norway was one of the couriers, who at the risk of his own life carried concealed messages across the Norwegian border into Sweden, where they could safely be relayed to the intelligence services of the Allies. In 1959 I heard Bishop Hagen describe his work. "We did not read the messages," he said. "We did not tamper with them or alter them. That was not our commission. Our sole task was to deliver messages composed by others. We were not asked to be original or imaginative. We were only asked to be faithful. We were to hand on a message as it had been handed on to us."

Jesus Christ is the Deed–Word of God. It is he and no one else—certainly no program or quadrennial emphasis—who has been anointed to preach good news to the poor, to proclaim release to the captives, recovery of sight to the blind, to set at liberty those who are oppressed, and to proclaim the acceptable year of the Lord. The Church has been commissioned, not to be original, but to witness to him. By spoken word, by sacrament, by service to others we point like John the Baptist to the Lamb of God who takes away the sins of the world. We have no other commission. "Woe to us if we do not preach the gospel!"

FOUR

The Protestant Minister and the Teaching Office of the Church

A symposium on the meaning of ordination appeared a few years ago in the *United Church Herald*. One of the contributors, a student from a seminary in the East, described ordination as setting out on a quest. The minister did not have all the answers to the questions that his people would raise, but together with his people, as a co-learner, he would seek answers to the meaning of life.

Humility is usually a virtue, but it is possible for humility to be misplaced. G. K. Chesterton posited a mythical people too humble to believe the multiplication table. It is humility for ministers to disavow that they have all the answers; but it is not humility to claim that they have no answers at all. The Church has received answers to the great questions of life that it did not cook up and that it has a responsibility to transmit. Ministers are ordained as bearers of the Church's gospel of a crucified Lord, however much their communication of that gospel may bear their own individual

63

stamp. Fundamental to the Protestant conception of the ministry is the conviction that the minister is a teacher in a church which is, to quote John Calvin, both mother and school.

Ministers are not ordained simply as teachers; some Protestant traditions emphasize other aspects of ministry more than the teaching office. Nevertheless, the teaching office is an indispensable function of the ordained ministry, even in the most charismatic traditions. Implicit in the structure and curriculum of almost any Protestant divinity school, liberal or conservative, is a doctrine of the minister as teacher. What that implies and how the office of teacher is related to the other functions of the ministry form the subject of this essay.

I

The ordained ministry was regarded by the early Church as a gift of God to the congregation and not simply as representative laity chosen by the congregation to perform certain special functions. The Church recognized, of course, that individual charismatic gifts were granted to all members of the Body of Christ and not simply to a select few. Every Christian received the Spirit at baptism and the Spirit equipped each Christian for service in the world. By the gifts granted through baptism each Christian shared in the unified ministry of Jesus Christ.

But the Spirit that grants differing gifts to each Christian in the Body of Christ also establishes the order that regulates that body. The charismatic ministry of the Church is not an unstructured ministry, even though that structure may appear at times to be rather loose. Offices are regarded as a gift of the Holy Spirit to the Church and there are important elements of church order in the New Testament that are of a quite primitive origin. That does not mean, however, that the actual development of church polity is simply the working out of a blueprint found in the New Testament or that there is no tension between the Pauline view of the Church and its later embodiment. But the principle at least seems to be clear: offices and order in the Church are regarded as gifts of the Holy Spirit.

Very early in the history of the Church the doctrine of the monarchical bishop developed. The bishop was the teacher of authentic Christian doctrine. Unity with the Catholic Church and membership in it were dependent on unity with a Catholic bishop by obedience to him. From a Catholic perspective the hierarchy is essential to the continued existence of the Church. The Catholic formula might be summarized as no bishop, no church; or at least no church in the full and proper sense of the term.

The Protestant Reformers rejected the idea that the Roman Catholic hierarchy is essential to the existence of the Church. But they did not reject the idea that offices and structure belong by divine ordination to the nature of the Church. Indeed, it is impossible to understand the origin of the Protestant Reformation without understanding Luther's high view of the office of a theological doctor. Luther was a medieval theological professor who had taken a vow in 1512 to defend the Church against false doctrine. Because of that vow and that office Luther felt that he bore a responsibility to speak out when he believed the gospel was being distorted. If he had only been a private individual, he might well have kept his peace and allowed himself to be meekly instructed by others. But since he was a teacher in the Church, he dared not keep silent. It was the medieval understanding of the office of a doctor and not the modern understanding of freedom of conscience that lies behind Luther's protest. Indeed, from one perspective the crisis of the Reformation may be understood as a crisis of confidence in the teaching office of the Church.

There is, however, a doubleness in Luther's doctrine of the ministry, an unresolved tension that Luther himself does very little to clarify. On the one hand, a Christian congregation has the right, divinely granted to it, to select its own pastor. In a sense the congregation antedates the ordained ministry and bestows on it the authority to perform certain functions on behalf of the Church and in its name. On the other hand, the pastor is the bearer of the very Word that antedates the Christian congregation and calls it into existence. There is, therefore, a sense in which the ordained ministry has received its authority to preach the gospel directly from God and prior to the creation of the congregation. Nevertheless, though ambiguities in Luther's doctrine of the ordained ministry exist, it is possible to conclude that Luther regards the office of the minister of Word and sacraments (including the teaching office) as essential to the life of the Church and not as an alien imposition on the life of the self-sufficient congregation that can get along well without the public proclamation of the Word and the administration of the sacraments.

The Congregationalists resolved Luther's dilemma by emphasizing the priority of the congregation. For Congregationalists, as for Presbyterians, the pastor is a bishop or teaching elder. However, unlike Catholics who argue no bishop, no church, the Congregationalists argued, no church, no bishop. The Church exists as a covenant community before a pastor is called. And a pastor can only be a pastor as pastor of some local congregation. For Catholics there cannot be a church, at least over the long haul, unless there is a hierarchy. For the Congregationalists there cannot be an ordained ministry unless there is first a church. The visible congregation is the fundamental reality. The pastor lives from that reality and is dependent for his office on it.

Even in this view of the Church, however, the congregation is incomplete—or, as the early Congregationalists would say, not "organical"—until it had called and ordained a pastor. Furthermore, the pastor, when he had been ordained, was not simply regarded as a functionary of the congregation. God, acting through the congregation, had bestowed on the minister the authority to proclaim the judgment and mercy of God to the congregation and, if necessary, in the face of its opposition. The proclamation of the Word of God and the teaching of authentic doctrine were not subject to the approval and ratification of the congregation. The minister in the exercise of his

67

office was endowed with an authority that had been entrusted to the congregation for only a brief time, so that the congregation in turn might delegate it to a called and ordained minister.

There is, in other words, a motif in church history that, however various its forms, recurs with remarkable persistence: although the whole people of God shares in the ministry of the Church in virtue of baptism, offices in the Church are to be regarded as gifts of the Holy Spirit. A church that lacks an ordained ministry is incomplete, precisely because it lacks one of the gifts of the Spirit. Though there are differences of opinion as to what offices are essential to the Church, there is at least agreement that the ministry of Word and sacrament belongs to that essential minimum.

II

While baptism is the ordination of all Christians for ministry in the world, ordination is the act of setting aside some Christians for public ministry to the Church. That does not mean that ordained clergy do not have a ministry to the world; they share in that ministry as do all other Christians in virtue of their baptism. That also does not mean that service to the Church may not involve the clergy in pioneering adventures outside the walls of the local parish. But it does mean that ordination is concerned principally with inner-churchly functions. The parish minister is, to use one of the titles associated by long tradition with the office of the pope, the *servus servorum dei,* the servant of the servants of God. The minister's function is to assist in equipping the people of God for their ministry to the world.

It would be an exaggeration to say that the laity have no inner-churchly functions to perform. There is a common priesthood of all of the faithful in which all Christians participate. This common priesthood has many aspects. When the Reformers, however, spoke of the priesthood of all believers, they referred principally to the right of all Christians to hear the confession of sin. Luther was not opposed to confession; he was opposed to making it a clerical monopoly. All Christians may hear confession and be bearers to one another of God's Word of judgment and grace. To be such a priest is to be Christ to the neighbor.

What all Christians may do privately, the ordained ministry has been set apart to do publicly. Ordained ministers do not differ from their parishioners in essence (as Roman Catholics maintain) but solely in function. The principal task of the layperson is mission to the world; the principal task of the clergy is mission to the Church.

III

The function of the ordained ministry is the public proclamation of the Word of God in its manifold forms to the congregation. Ordination is for the purpose of preaching, teaching, and administering the sacraments. Anyone who has been ordained to the ministry of the Church but who no longer is occupied with the public service of Word and sacraments is no longer performing the function for which he or she was ordained. Ordination is not a general commissioning for the service of God; that is the purpose of baptism. Ordination is so indissolubly linked to the service of Word and sacraments that it is meaningless apart from them.

In the Roman Catholic tradition ordination is directed specifically toward the sacrament of the eucharist. Preaching has not been regarded as the principal function of the ordained ministry and theology is less central to the life of the local Catholic parish than among Protestants. Grace is given to the faithful through sacraments rather than through homilies, though homilies perform an important task of theological and moral instruction.

The Protestant Reformers, however, redefine the role of the ministry in terms of the proclamation and teaching of the Word of God. The sermon is not merely doctrinal instruction or moral exhortation. It is a means of grace. From a Catholic perspective the sermon has now become a sacrament. God speaks through human language and through human words effects those changes in the human condition that Catholic theology restricts to the power of the sacraments.

IV

The offices of preaching, teaching, and discipline are inseparable from the single office of the ministry of the Word of God. The Reformed tradition made the most elaborate attempt to separate the ministry of the Word into four distinct offices: teacher, pastor, elder, and deacon. According to Reformed theology the teacher was responsible for explaining the meaning of Scripture and its theological and ethical implications, though without resorting to exhortation or rhetorical appeals for decision (a description that badly characterizes the work of any decent teacher, regardless of the discipline). A pastor also teaches, but differs from the teacher with respect to the mode or manner of his teaching. Unlike the teacher, the preacher is expected to use rhetorical arts to move his listeners to decision or action. Discipline is exercised by the pastor together with a group of lay elders. The poor are cared for by the lay deacons of the congregation. The division of labor is logical, admirable, but also artificial.

Everything in Protestant theology comes back to the multifaceted character of the Word of God. The Word teaches, nurtures, moves to decision, judges, disciplines, and encourages. It must find expression in works of charity or it remains only the letter that kills. Wherever the Word of God is proclaimed it does all four offices: teaches, exhorts, disciplines, and moves to acts of charity. Even the Sunday school, which ostensibly separates the office of preaching at 11:00 A.M. from the office of teaching at 9:30 A.M., combines teaching with lay preaching, worship, and discipline. The Word of God cannot be compartmentalized, even though one may for a brief period of time emphasize one aspect of the Word more than another. Teaching is a legitimate activity of the Church, but one can never rule out in advance the possibility that the taught may be converted to the teaching, may

71

assimilate the teaching in worship and prayer, or may respond to the teaching by an act of compassion for another in distress. The ministry of the Word of God is finally indivisible.

V

The Reformers understood the discharge of the office of minister as the faithful transmission of the Word entrusted to the ordinand. Christian ministers are not free-lance religious prophets, however much the work of the ministry may involve the concrete proclamation of God's judgment and grace. Nor are they *homines religiosi*, people more sensitive than their fellows to religious values, more quickly overcome than they with the mystery and wonder of existence. The work of the minister is rather prosaic in comparison with these more romantic notions of the meaning of ministry. To be a minister is, to put it bluntly, to be a servant and the virtue most highly prized in a servant is not originality, but fidelity. Ministers have been ordained to transmit a message that they did not compose and that they dare not alter. They have been called, not to improvise their assignment, but fulfill a role prescribed for them by someone else.

Fidelity in their calling does not mean, of course, that ministers pass on everything they receive. Ministers are not curators of outdated techniques. They are not echo chambers in which every voice that claims the attention of the Church may resonate unhindered. Fidelity does not exclude discrimination. The faithful minister is not one who passes on unchallenged everything that he or she receives in the Church. The faithful minister is the one who hears the voice of the Shepherd through the cacophonous clamor of all the voices speaking to and for the Church. "He who hears the Word of God," said Thomas á Kempis, "is freed from a multitude of opinions." Not everything we receive should be passed on. True fidelity is fidelity to Christ, not to the past *per se*.

Furthermore, faithful transmission does not do away with the necessity of interpretation. If ministers pass on what they receive without further interpretation, they may pass on something quite different from what they received. Theological formulations require interpretation if their intention is to be preserved.

It is a principle of Protestant theology that God comes to men and women as they are and not as he would like them to be. That means that God reveals himself before men and women are ready to receive him. Not only the moral life of men and women but also their intellectual life is unprepared for the divine self-manifestation. God takes the human race by surprise; he comes when men and women are least ready for him.

This means that theologies have a mixed character. They are partly true and partly false. Talk about God is a human enterprise, and like every other human enterprise is marked by finitude, error, and sin. That does not mean that the Church's talk about God is so relative that it has no authority at all or that the Church is so humble that it no longer believes that it is witnessing about a matter that makes the difference between life and death. It does not mean that the Church surrenders its age-old claim to be led by the Spirit. But the presence of the Holy Spirit in the Church does not mean that the Church is infallible any more than it guarantees that the Church is without sin. The Holy Spirit is a pledge, a down payment. The Spirit guarantees that the Church will some day be without error as it will some day be without sin. But at the moment the Church stands under the sign of "not yet." It has and it does not have. It is a deceiver, yet true.

The Church makes mistakes, but it also tells the truth. In spite of its finitude, sin, narrow-mindedness, and error, God works through it in the world, calling men and women into fellowship with himself. The Church's witness, its theology, its testimony are all human. It has its treasure in earthen vessels; it only knows in part. But the fact that the Church sins does not cancel out the reality of its claim to be the people of God; and the fact that the Church errs does not cancel out the truth of its proclamation that Jesus Christ is Lord and Redeemer. The treasure is in an earthen vessel, but it is real treasure.

VI

In witnessing to the truth the Church dare not simply repeat without interpretation the formulae of the past. Robert Chiles in his book, *Theological Transition in American Methodism, 1790–1935,* gives a striking example of the way in which theological affirmations can have a markedly different meaning in different historical circumstances. Wesley protested against the eighteenth-century Calvinist doctrine of predestination in the name of the freedom and sovereignty of divine grace. He argued that God was not the prisoner of a divine decree but was free to be gracious to whomever he would be gracious. In other words, God was free to be gracious to the whole human race. Wesley stressed the freedom and sovereignty of God's merciful activity.

In the nineteenth century, however, there was a subtle shift of emphasis in Methodist theology. Wesley stressed the freedom of God's grace. Later Methodists, while citing Wesley copiously, stressed the freedom of the human will. What was a theological point for Wesley became an anthropological point for his followers. Wesley argued that God can be gracious to any penitent but that men and women cannot come to God until moved by divine grace. His followers argued that human beings are free moral agents and that God's grace cannot overcome the sovereign freedom of the human will. The formulae are much the same but the point is fundamentally different.

Fidelity to one's calling as an ordained minister of Word and sacraments means that one must free oneself from the disposition to take every theological affirmation from the past literally. Some can, and should, be taken literally, but not all. The Latin and Greek Fathers worked with metaphysical categories and with philosophical assumptions that we do not share. If we take literally many of the things they said, we would be forced to reject them. But rejection is a sign of failure of nerve; it is a sign of the inability or unwillingness to penetrate beneath the culturally conditioned statement of a doctrine to its intention. Repeating a formula from the past without translation is very much like repeating a statement from a foreign language without translation. Its meaning has been lost, not because it is meaningless in itself, but because its meaning has not been translated into terms that are meaningful to us.

Many times the past speaks to us directly without the aid of a conscious act of interpretation. But many times it does not. If we repeat what we have received without making its meaning clear, we have failed to discharge our office responsibly. We are to deliver what we also received. But that act of delivery involves us in interpretation. Repetition without interpretation may be a sign, not of fidelity, but of incompetence.

The difficulty with the image of the minister as a messenger is that the minister is not merely a messenger. Every minister is also a witness. Ministers are claimed by the very message that they proclaim. There is in all Christian proclamation the Wesleyan note: "What we have seen and heard with confidence we tell." There is in preaching always the note of witness: "Come, see a man who told me all that I ever did. Can this be the Christ?"

In a sense this aspect of Christian proclamation is the most embarrassing. People who are honest with themselves would not want the credibility of the gospel to be measured solely by the impact of that gospel on their own lives. Yet there is no way to escape from the element of witness by compartmentalizing life. The gospel that is preached lays claim to the whole of life and something is fundamentally wrong with a proclamation of the good news that is untouched by it. The preacher is a witness who claims to know the reality of which he or she speaks otherwise than by hearsay. Ministers are not simply messengers and teachers. They are witnesses, people grasped by the power of what they proclaim.

Yet the original image is still valid. Christian ministers are not merely witnesses; they are also messengers. They have been commissioned by the Church, not to give their own testimony, but to carry its message. And that message is valid, whether or not Protestant ministers believe it, whether or not they profit from it, whether or not they enjoy it. The power and truth of the message are quite independent of the personal faith of the messenger who delivers it. It is God's counsel and promise that ministers declare, not their own, and God is truthful, though every human being be false.

The late Carl Michalson of Drew used to suggest to his classes that they ought to preach the faith of the Church even if they could not claim the whole of that faith for themselves. The Church, he said, lives from the Word of God; it cannot live from heresy. Though what Michalson recommended sounded like theological novelty to his students, he was actually doing nothing more than reaffirming the position of the Church against the Donatists. The Word and sacraments of the Church are not the minister's personal property. Ministers have no right to deny them to their parishioners simply because they find no life in them for themselves nor does their unfaith invalidate that Word and those sacraments.

We were horrified, as I recall, by Michalson's suggestion. It seemed to us like hypocrisy to speak a Word that we had not made our own, perhaps could not. In the American tradition we equated preaching with the affirmation of personal religious experience. We grasped the witness element of preaching; we understood it subjectively. But we did not grasp the *extra nos* dimension; we did not grasp the objectivity of God's Word and work outside us. God is doing his work in the world whether we participate in it or not, whether we understand it or not, whether we feel it or not. It is not through our religious experience that God brings life and healing to the world, though our experience may confirm for us the objectivity of God's working. It is by his Word and sacraments that God brings men and women into fellowship with himself, apart from our religious experience and even, perhaps, in spite of it.

VII

Responsibility for the faithful transmission of the gospel is corporate. Among the radical reformers that responsibility was characteristically exercised by the local congregation of believers. Pilgrim Marpeck, for example, makes it clear that deviant interpretations of the Bible are best corrected in a group discussion with other laypeople who have met the moral demands of the New Testament and paid the cost of discipleship. The Lutheran and Reformed traditions, on the other hand, have generally appealed to synods and councils as the place to reconcile conflicts over the meaning of the Bible. The controversy in Holland, for example, between the Reformed Orthodox and the followers of James Arminius was settled by the Reformed equivalent of an ecumenical council held at Dordrecht in 1618. Even United Methodists, who have bishops, rely, not on bishops, but on the elders of an annual conference to certify new ordinands and to provide for the orderly transmission of the gospel from one generation to another. It could be argued that one of the chief differences between Protestants and Roman Catholics is that Catholics assign principal responsibility for the faithful transmission of the gospel to bishops while Protestants assign it either to presbyters in synod (the magisterial Reformation) or to the local congregation of the laity (the radical Reformation).

VIII

The faithful transmission of the Word of God commits the church to the provision of a learned ministry. The Reformers did not affirm the right of private judgment. There were, to be sure, radical reformers who believed that the Bible in the hands of a plowboy instructed by the Holy Spirit was better and more to be trusted than what a learned pastor or teacher taught them. But this was a minority position.

The Reformers envisioned a learned ministry, gifted persons set apart by the Church for the study of Holy Scripture, for the study of theology, for the study of the Fathers. This learned ministry not only preached to the laity but also produced confessions that were meant to be guides for young Christians and for those less learned, to lead them by clear paths into the meaning of Holy Scripture. The Reformers did not believe that any person's opinion was as good as anyone else's or that it made no difference what one believed as long as one was sincere. The meaning of Holy Scripture was too important for the Church to treat it so casually. Pastors and teachers were given to the Church for its edification.

What the Reformers did reject was the doctrine of implicit faith. There is a sense, of course, in which the Reformation retained a doctrine of implicit faith. To be committed to the Christian faith does not mean that one understands every mystery of that faith. There is a sense in which one believes implicitly what one does not understand. What the Reformers rejected was the idea that the laity, because they are instructed by pastors and teachers, have no theological responsibility of their own. One cannot simply say, "I believe what the Church teaches," and assume that one has thereby discharged one's responsibility to understand the Christian faith. On the contrary, every layperson has the responsibility to understand his or her faith. That does not mean that every layperson is a teacher of others, though the gift of teaching may be given to a layperson as well as to a pastor. But it does imply that laypeople seek to understand what it means to be Christian, what demands are laid upon them by God and what is given to them in the gospel. Not private judgment but the theological responsibility of the whole people of God is the thrust of the Protestant movement.

IX

To sum up, then, one may say that there are certain elements in the Protestant tradition concerning the teaching office of the Church that are still important for our consideration: (1) although the whole people of God shares in the ministry of the Church by virtue of baptism, offices in the Church are to be regarded as a gift of the Holy Spirit; (2) while baptism is the ordination of all Christians for ministry in the world, ordination is the act of setting aside some Christians for public ministry to the Church; (3) the function of the ordained ministry is the public proclamation of the Word of God in its manifold forms to the congregation; (4) the offices of preaching, teaching, and discipline are inseparable from the single office of the ministry of the Word of God; (5) the discharge of the office of a minister is the faithful transmission of the Word that has been entrusted to the Church; (6) the minister in transmitting this Word is both a messenger and a witness; (7) responsibility for the faithful transmission of the Word is corporate; and (8) the faithful transmission of the Word of God commits the Church to the provision of a learned ministry.

81

FIVE

Asbury's Doctrine of Ministry

Studies of the meaning of ordination in the Wesleyan tradition have appealed, as such studies should, to the biblical, historical, and practical dimensions of the problem. Biblical studies over the last twenty years have clarified many of the problems of Church order in the New Testament and have made it apparent to all that pluriformity in the Church's order and structure belongs to the earliest decades of the Church's life and is not a later development. Similarly, Wesley's understanding of ordination with its slow and painful development and its unresolved ambiguities has been discussed at some length by such divergent commentators as Franz Hildebrandt and Frank Baker.

Yet in all these discussions of ordination and ministry in the Wesleyan tradition, little, if any, reference has been made to the role of Francis Asbury in shaping the theology of ordination and the understanding of ministry among the early Methodists in America. The reasons for this neglect are understandable. While Asbury was Wesley's equal in administrative gifts and his superior in understanding the unique situation posed by the American frontier, he was clearly Wesley's inferior as a theologian. Furthermore, Asbury, while not slavishly dependent on Wesley's opinions and willing to oppose him in matters of strategy, certainly did not intend to deviate at any point from the Wesleyan standards of doctrine. It could conceivably be argued that Asbury's theology is nothing more than a homespun and simplified copy of Wesley's.

Still there are differences. Though Asbury was an avid reader of theology all his life and even learned Hebrew while on horseback, he was not university trained and lacked the university-trained concern with the delicate shades of less and more. Decisions that were difficult for Wesley and were arrived at only after a long and painful process of setting aside dearly held beliefs were relatively easy for Asbury to assent to. The break with Anglicanism, once it was deemed necessary, was quick, clean, and without tears. Asbury had the plain man's interest in conclusions, not the scholar's fascination with arguments. If it must be, so be it. Asbury was even more consistent than Wesley in drawing out the implications of Wesley's decision to ordain, much to Wesley's own discomfiture and annoyance. Of all the characters in Bunyan's *Pilgrim's Progress* who bear no resemblance to Francis Asbury, he was least like Mr. Ready-to-halt.

For nearly forty-five years (from Sunday, October 27, 1771, when Francis Asbury arrived in

83

Philadelphia from Bristol, England, until Sunday, March 31, 1816, when he died in Spottsylvania, Virginia) he made his impact felt on the American scene. He enforced discipline in Philadelphia, even if it resulted in a temporary loss of membership and was opposed by certain of the other ministers. He restrained his fellow workers from the administration of the sacraments, with one exception, until the separation with Anglicanism occurred and then he defended the validity of Methodist orders against all comers. His vision of the ministry, most fully elaborated in his valedictory address to Bishop McKendree, written in Lancaster, Pennsylvania, on August 5, 1813, was indelibly imprinted on the early Methodist conferences, even in the face of the O'Kelly schism.

Wesley's understanding of ordination had been colored by his Anglican upbringing. When Wesley left for America as a missionary, he believed firmly in the historic episcopate and apostolic succession, even to the extent of denying the validity of baptisms performed by non-episcopally ordained clergy. The Lutherans had no right to celebrate the eucharist. Only Anglican (and, of course, Roman Catholic) priests had received valid ordinations.

How Wesley changed his mind is too long and complicated a story to be told here. He came to believe, after reading Lord Peter King's *An Enquiry into the Constitution, Discipline, Unity and Worship of the Primitive Church,* that presbyters and bishops do not differ in order, but only in degree. That is to say, that both bishops and presbyters have the same right to celebrate the Lord's Supper and to ordain,

84

but in the interest of good order in the Church the right to ordain, which belongs to every presbyter, has been restricted in its exercise to the bishop. Nevertheless, in an emergency situation presbyters can ordain and can even consecrate a duly elected presbyter as bishop. The notion of apostolic succession Wesley abandoned as a myth. There is no single scriptural polity in the sense that one form of church government and it alone is prescribed by Scripture. Still in all, the Anglican polity of bishops, presbyters, and deacons is scriptural, in the sense that it is compatible with scriptural principles.

Wesley remained true to the Anglican tradition in his separation of the ministry of the Word, which could be carried on by lay preachers, and the ministry of the sacraments, which could only be performed by ministers who were properly ordained. Laymen can preach, deacons can preach and baptize, and elders or presbyters can preach, baptize, and celebrate Communion.

While Wesley claimed the authority of King, and also of Stillingfleet, for the ordination of Coke as superintendent and his companions as clergy for the American church, he did not follow the pattern recommended by them. He did not seek the majority decision of the English Methodist ministers, much less that of the American Methodists, before ordaining Coke. In a sense Wesley ordained without the explicit consent of the Methodist Church and therefore ordained on his own authority. He substituted Wesleyan succession for apostolic succession. This was a state of affairs that

Asbury found disagreeable and one that he did not permit to be repeated in his own ordination to the episcopacy. Indeed, one may well ask whether Coke arrived in America as anything more than a presbyter of the Church of England. Certainly, he was not a bishop in Anglican eyes. It is doubtful whether he was one on Methodist principles either.

Asbury's understanding of ordination was much less nuanced but far more consistent than Wesley's. The threefold pattern of bishops, elders, and deacons is the pattern for the government of the Church prescribed in Scripture. The bishops are the successors of the apostles and carry on their ministry of itinerant evangelism. All three orders have the right to preach, and both elders and bishops have the right to celebrate the Lord's Supper. As far as their sacramental function is concerned—and the sacramental aspect of ordination is the aspect that least interested Asbury— bishops and elders are equal.

Yet there is a more fundamental sense in which bishops and elders are not equal. The bishop has been set apart both to serve as the *pastor pastorum* and as the overseer of the Church's ministry. Since ordination to the office of a bishop is ordination to a permanent status, barring abuse of the office, the bishop is a permanent chairman of the conference of elders and their perpetual overseer. As regards the proclamation of the gospel, all preachers are on the same level, whether lay or ordained. As regards the celebration of the sacraments, all elders and bishops are on the same plane. But as regards the exercise of disciplinary authority in the Church, the bishop is on a permanently higher plane than the presbyters. One must also conclude, especially in view of the O'Kelly schism, that the bishop is superior to the conference as well. Asbury observed in his Journal.

> I recollect having read, some years since, Ostervald's Christian Theology: having a wish to transcribe a few sentiments in the work, I met with it, and extracted from chap. 2, page 317, what follows. "Yet it cannot be denied that in the primitive Church there was always a president who presided over others, who were in a state of equality with himself: this is clearly proved from the catalogues of bishops to be found in Eusebius and others; in them we may see the names of the bishops belonging to the principal Churches, many of whom were ordained whilst the apostles (but especially John) were still living." So far Mr. Ostervald, who, I presume was a Presbyterian. In Cave's Lives of the Fathers, and in the writings of the ancients, it will appear that the Churches of Alexandria, and elsewhere, had large congregations, many elders; that the apostles might appoint and ordain bishops. Mr. Ostervald, who, it appears, is a candid and well-informed man, has gone as far as might be expected for a Presbyterian. For myself, I see but a hair's breadth difference between the sentiments of the respectable and learned author of Christian Theology, and the practice of the Methodist Episcopal Church. There is not—nor indeed, in my mind, can there be—a perfect equality between a constant president, and those over whom he always presides.[1]

That is not to say that all *episkope*, all disciplinary authority in the Church, resides in the person of

the bishop. Discipline and authority are shared by
elders, deacons, lay preachers, exhorters, class
leaders—indeed, by all officers. But in all disputed
matters the final decision is the bishop's. He is not
the sole authority, but as permanent president he is
the highest.

Immediately after his consecration as superintendent (which Coke, Asbury, and Charles Wesley
understood to be an ordination as bishop, even if
John Wesley was reluctant to use the term), Asbury
donned the vestments of an Anglican bishop. He
quickly removed them again when they provoked
unfavorable comment and jokes among the
rough-hewn frontier preachers. Nevertheless, the
use of the vestments signifies that Asbury understood his election and consecration to be ordination
to the office of a bishop, a successor of the apostles,
with as much right—in Asbury's mind, more
right—to wear the vestments of a bishop than any
sedentary bishop of the Church of England.

When his authority as bishop was challenged,
Asbury appealed to a fivefold base:

> I will tell the world what I rest my authority upon.
> 1. Divine authority. 2. Seniority in America. 3. The
> election of the General Conference. 4. My ordina-
> tion by Thomas Coke, William Philip Otterbein,
> German Presbyterian minister, Richard Whatcoat,
> and Thomas Vasey. 5. Because the signs of an
> apostle have been seen in me.[2]

Divine authority—the office of a bishop is
scriptural, however much the Presbyterians may
deny it or the Anglicans misunderstand it.

Seniority in America—the bishop was the father in God of many of the preachers in the Methodist connection, quite apart from his election to be their overseer. Even without election and consecration, he had a certain claim on the loyalty of the Methodist itinerants.

The election of the General Conference—no one could accuse Asbury of the same shaky basis for his consecration as bishop as Coke must claim for his. The conference had consented to his ordination. The elders had chosen one of their number as bishop as it was their inherent and primitive right to do.

Ordination by Coke, Otterbein, Whatcoat, and Vasey—no Presbyterian could argue with the legitimacy of Asbury's ordination nor could any Episcopalian who accepted the theories of King and Stillingfleet. It was as good a Presbyterian ordination as any Reformed Church could offer; as good an Episcopalian ordination as the primitive Church had given.

The signs of an apostle—here is the Wesleyan note. *Medicus non est qui non medetur.* The physician is known by his cures. Apostolic succession is not conferred by digital contact with an Anglican bishop. The only succession that matters is succession in apostolic doctrine and practice. And the mark of apostolic succession is, as some wag once noted, apostolic success. Who had more right to be called a bishop? The Anglican divine sipping port in his palace after a leisurely afternoon of calling at the salons of his wealthier parishioners or the rugged son of a Staffordshire gardener

89

crossing the Appalachians on a pony in order to preach at some remote farmhouse in Virginia? The sign of apostolicity is to be under orders and not merely in them.

Asbury concurred with Wesley's pointed questions to the Anglican bishop who took "unfashionable pains" to examine his candidates for Holy Orders:

Examining them! In what respects? Why, whether they understand a little *Latin* and *Greek* and can answer a few trite questions in the science of divinity! Alas, how little does this avail! Does your Lordship examine whether they serve *Christ* or *Belial*? whether they love God or the world? whether they ever had any serious thoughts about heaven or hell? whether they have any real desire to save their own souls or the souls of others? If not, what have they to do with Holy Orders? and what will become of the souls committed to their care?[3]

The chief mark of the apostolicity of the Methodist episcopate was its itinerant character. It was Asbury's contention that the bishops were the successors of the apostles and therefore like them were itinerant evangelists. It was not until the second century that bishops became identified with one diocese, that—to use the Methodist technical term—they "located." This location of bishops marks the fall of the episcopate from its former glory. So far from regarding the Anglican episcopate as complete with the Methodist a pale imitation of it, Asbury believed the exact reverse to be true. Authentic episcopacy, lost for centuries, has now been restored in the polity of the Methodist Church. Like the apostles, and unlike the Greeks, Latins, and Anglicans, Methodist bishops are itinerants.

> I am bold to say that the apostolic order of things was lost in the first century, when Church governments were adulterated and had much corruption attached to them. At the Reformation, the reformers only beat off a part of the rubbish, which put a stop to the rapid increase of absurdities at that time; but how they have increased since! Recollect the state of the different Churches, as it respects government and discipline, in the seventeenth century when the Lord raised up that great and good man, John Wesley, who formed an evangelical society in England. In 1784, an apostolical form of Church government was formed in the United States of America at the first General Conference of the Methodist Episcopal Church held at Baltimore, in the State of Maryland.[4]

While itinerancy was essential to the nature of authentic episcopacy, celibacy belonged to its *bene esse*. It may be embarrassing to realize that the first bishop of the Methodist Church was not only a bachelor, but even defended celibacy and urged his presbyters to imitate him (as he imitated Paul) in pursuing a celibate life. It was not possible to carry out the functions of authentic episcopacy with a wife and family. The man who marries must assume his family obligations. He cannot really fulfill the obligations of itinerancy. Asbury was not opposed to marriage for laity, but was convinced that it was not a suitable state for Methodist preachers. His journal is full of wry comments about preachers he lost either to the devil or to the women. Family life means location, the settled parish, Presbyterianism (in church government if not in doctrine!).

> Marriage is honourable in all—but to me it is a ceremony awful as death. Well may it be so, when I calculate we have lost the travelling labours of two hundred of the best men in America, or the world, by marriage and consequent location.[5]

While one can construct a fully developed theory of the episcopate from Asbury's journal and letters, it is more difficult to describe the role of the elder and deacon. They share in the same ministry of Word and sacraments, but differ principally in the degree of authority that they exercise.

Laity, of course, are not represented at the level of the conference. The government of the church is in the hands of the traveling preachers. The ministry appoints the ministry. That is the Methodist via media between the Anglican delegation of sacramental authority from the bishop to the elders and the conferral of authority on the minister by the laity in Congregationalist polity. If a layman wishes to share in the government of the church, let him become a traveling preacher!

There is not time to question Asbury about his understanding of the episcopate—to ask, for example, in what way the understanding of the episcopate proposed by the Consultation on Church Union corrects Asbury's teaching or needs to be corrected by him. There is only time to summarize his understanding of the ministry as a necessary prologue to that further discussion.

1. The threefold ministry of bishops, elders, and deacons is the New Testament pattern.

2. The authority of the Methodist ministry was not conferred on it by the people called Methodists, but was conferred through already existing ministries. Through Coke the Methodist ministry stands in succession to the Anglican Mother Church; through Otterbein it is linked to the Continental Reformation. The ministry appoints the ministry.

3. Bishops, elders, and deacons share in the ministry of Word and sacrament. All share equally in the ministry of the Word; deacons only partially in the ministry of the sacraments.

4. Bishops differ from elders solely in administrative authority.

5. The office of a bishop is a permanent office. He is not merely an elder who returns to his place among the other elders when his term of office is completed.

6. Bishops are successors of the apostles and therefore must discharge the function of an itinerant evangelist. Itinerancy belongs to the *esse* of the episcopate, while it belongs only to the *bene esse* of the office of elder or deacon.

7. The first Methodist elders were ordained by Anglican and Reformed elders, since elders have the inherent right to ordain.

8. These elders then consecrated one of their number as permanent president or bishop.

9. The validity of Methodist orders is proven by the success of the Methodist Church in the

discharge of its mission to convert the unconverted and to spread scriptural holiness. They are a people whom God owns.

Churches that have a Presbyterian or Congregationalist form of government may find the Wesleyan understanding of episcopacy fully as objectionable as the older Anglican or Roman Catholic positions, since, in the Reformed tradition, the presbyter is already a bishop and no further episcopal office is wanted. Anglicans, who struggle with ambiguities in their own tradition on the episcopacy, may shudder at the thought of taking on any of the ambiguities in the Wesleyan tradition and may well join Roman Catholics in deploring the loss of certain pastoral and sacramental dimensions of the historic episcopate in the episcopal office instituted by Asbury.

Nevertheless, although there are substantial objections that can be lodged against Asbury's conception of the ministry by episcopal and non-episcopal churches alike, his conception has in one form or another been institutionalized in the episcopal wing of the Wesleyan tradition. Ecumenical discussions of the historic episcopate with representatives of the Wesleyan tradition will not get very far unless the non–Wesleyan partners in those discussions are aware that the word "bishop" conjures up in the Wesleyan mind associations and theological assumptions initiated by Asbury and nurtured in a Free Church environment.

However much the episcopal office may be altered in any future union of churches across denominational lines, one note in Asbury's view

dare not, I think, be lost without general impover-
ishment. That is the connection in his theology and
practice between episcopacy and mission. According to the pastoral epistles, Paul charged the young
bishop, Timothy, to do the work of an evangelist. It
is a charge that Asbury heard and obeyed. Church
order is not an end in itself. The realignment of the
internal structures of moribund institutions represents no great gain for the world. Only if
ecclesiastical offices are subordinate to the mission
of the gospel can they properly be discharged. The
work of an itinerant evangelist may not be the first
duty of a bishop and it is certainly not the only duty;
but it is nevertheless an indispensable task of any
"scriptural" bishop.

NOTES

1. Elmer T. Clark, ed., *The Journal and Letters of Francis Asbury*, vol. II (Nashville: Abingdon Press, 1958), pp. 289-90.
2. Ibid., pp. 469-70.
3. John Telford, ed., *The Letters of the Rev. John Wesley* (London: Epworth Press, 1931).
4. Clark, *The Journal and Letters of Francis Asbury*, vol. III, pp. 475-76.
5. Ibid., vol. II, p. 474.

SIX

Theological Reflections on the Reformation and the Status of Women

The role of women in the Reformation has become an increasingly popular subject for research during the last decade. Historians have always been fascinated with the role of political figures such as Elizabeth I or her sister, Mary Tudor, in the formation of the character and institutions of Protestant Christianity in England. Catherine de Medici and Marguerite d'Angoulême in France, while less well known than their English counterparts, have nevertheless received considerable attention in scholarly journals and books. The poetry of Vittoria Colonna in Italy, the mystical writings of St. Teresa of Avila in Spain, and the polemical tracts of Katherine Zell in Alsace made individually and together an important impact on the development of popular religious beliefs in Europe in the sixteenth century. Even the women who are remembered primarily for the men whom they married have left their own impress on the history of the Reformation era, from Katherina von Bora, whose tightfisted management of the financial affairs of the Luther household has become legendary, to the quiet Wibrandis Rosenblatt, who had the unusual distinction of marrying in succession three of the most important reformers: Johann Oecolampadius, Wolfgang Capito, and Martin Bucer.

Women made a significant contribution to the spread and establishment of the Protestant Reformation, even if they did not (with very few exceptions) write commentaries on Scripture, occupy important European pulpits, or compose technical essays in theology. But the reverse proposition is also true: the Reformation, both in its ideology and in combination with other social forces, effected a change in the status of European women. The implications of what took place then are worth considering as we ponder the respective roles of men and women in Church and society today.

I

The Council of Florence in 1439 declared officially that marriage was a sacrament and that it bestowed a triple good. (1) The procreation of children, by which was meant not simply the biological act of reproduction but also the nurture and education of children for a productive role in society. This control of sexual drives within structures that took responsibility for the personal and biological effects of sexual intercourse provided, to use the quaint but painfully accurate phrase, "a remedy for concupiscence." (2) Mutual society, which was generally interpreted to mean a perpetual monogamous covenant between a man and a woman, one which emphasized fidelity and trust over the fluctuations of feeling and passion. (3) Indissolubility. As Christ loved the Church with a commitment that never fails, so men and women were to love one another and to rear their children in the love and fear of God. Such love implies mutual sacrifice and devotion and excludes from the outset all possibility of divorce. Only if Christ can be separated from the Church can the marriage bond between husband and wife be dissolved.

While the late medieval Church exalted the institution of marriage in language that can scarcely be surpassed, it also praised virginity as a higher moral state and required its clergy to be celibate. Though some late medieval figures, such as Nicholas de Blony, taught that marriage was as meritorious as celibacy, the majority of late medieval clergy agreed with the opinion of the famous Strassburg preacher, John Geiler of Kaysersberg, who observed that marriage is honorable but not preferable to the state of celibacy.

There were, after all, in the Bible plenty of sayings that lent support to the development of a celibate ethic. Paul had indicated that celibacy was preferable to marriage, not because of a general world-weariness, but because the celibate minister was delivered from family cares and responsibilities and was therefore free to be devoted completely to the work of the gospel. Jesus had praised those disciples who became eunuchs for the kingdom of heaven, even though it is impossible to regard Jesus as an ascetic in the ordinary sense of the term. And after the triumph of Christianity in Europe, celibacy was one of the few forms of martyrdom still accessible to the grandchildren of Cyprian and Perpetua.

The celibate ethic was reinforced by a distinction between commands and counsels. Commands are ethical requirements binding on all Christians, such as the prohibition of murder or adultery. Counsels, on the other hand, are moral requirements binding on an elite within the Church who have obligated themselves by a vow to a more rigorous standard of Christian discipleship. Among the counsels are the sayings of Jesus on non-retaliation, the renunciation of private property, and the desirability of a celibate life. Ever since canon 33 of the Council of Elvira (ca. 300) clerical celibacy had been enjoined in the West, though the Anglo-Saxon Church in Britain had a married clergy. The laity, however, were only required to keep the commandments concerning adultery and fornication.

The celibate ethic received important encouragement from the writings and example of Augustine, who could find for himself no middle ground between ascetism and sexual license. Augustine taught that original sin was transmitted from generation to generation not by the sexual act itself (that would be Manichaean), but by the inordinate self-regard of the sexual partners who think of themselves more highly than they ought to think and who seek their own good rather than the good of their spouses. Biology was not the culprit, though original sin was connected with human sexual activity in the broader sense. While the celibate Christian did not participate in the admitted goods of marriage, the celibate was also free of responsibility for its unfortunate side effects.

The emphasis on celibacy as the preferred state for the serious Christian and the obligation of the clergy to remain celibate created a permanent class of men not fully integrated into society. Because the clergy had no wives and family of their own, they were regarded by the suspicious laity (and not always unjustly) as a perpetual threat to the stability of the home. Instances of anticlerical sentiment relating to the alleged sexual offenses of some of the clergy are all too easy to find in the sources.

In 1519 a group of canons in Strassburg, returning from a drunken party, were attacked by a group of citizens who regarded them as a danger to the moral purity of their wives and daughters. John Murner, brother of the rabidly anti-feminist Franciscan friar, Thomas Murner, accused the canons of Young St. Peter's Church in Strassburg of seducing his sister. In January of 1520 two women charged three members of the clergy, including the vicar of the Strassburg cathedral, with breaking into their homes at midnight and making improper sexual advances. When the women resisted, they were beaten. Needless to say, the guilty clergy were fined and imprisoned by the Strassburg city council.

Even the confessional was regarded with suspicion by the laity. The Eisenach preacher, Jacob Strauss, attacked the confessional practice of the late medieval clergy as profoundly unsettling to the peace and stability of Christian family life.

> In the confessional simple folk learn things about sin and evil which have never occurred to them before, and which need not ever have occurred to them! The confessional is a schooling in sin. It is known and many thousands can attest how often mischievous and perverse monks out of their shameless hearts have so thoroughly and persistently questioned young girls and boys, innocent children, and simple wives about the sins of the flesh in their cursed confessional corners that more harm was done there to Christian chasteness and purity than in any whorehouse in the world. He is considered a good father confessor who can probe into every secret recess of the heart and instill into the innocent penitent every sin his flesh has not yet experienced. They want to know from virtuous wives all the circumstances of the marital duty—how their husbands do it [certain "unnatural positions" were very serious sins], how often, how much pleasure it brings, when it is done, and the like. In this way new desires and lusts are stimulated within the weak. They even teach poor wives not to submit to their husbands on certain holidays and during Lent.[1]

If clergy were regarded by the laity as a threat to the stability of the home, women were regarded by clergy as a threat to their celibacy and moral purity. Sebastian Brant, himself a layman, gave expression

101

to this sentiment when he wrote his masterpiece, *The Ship of Fools* (1494):

> Who sees too much of women's charms
> His morals and his conscience harms;
> He cannot worship God aright
> Who finds in women great delight.[2]

In a time of moral decline and disintegration (and Brant like Geiler of Kaysersberg was convinced that he lived in such a time of moral decay), the "frailty" of women constitutes a perpetual temptation for a celibate clergy, whose vows require them to abstain from sexual activity, but whose vocation brings them in constant contact with the wives and daughters of laymen. Not all clergy were able to resist the temptations strewn in their path. Friar Martin Luther, O.E.S.A., had no difficulty keeping his celibate vows; Father Huldrych Zwingli and Friar Martin Bucer, O.P., were not so morally heroic.

Many clergy took concubines, a practice winked at by some ecclesiastical superiors and even taxed by a few bishops as a way of raising additional revenue for the diocese. The Protestant reformer Heinrich Bullinger was born into such a clerical "family." But clergy who took concubines rather than place themselves in the path of a temptation that they did not trust themselves to resist placed themselves in another kind of moral dilemma. The relationship between a priest and his housekeeper, however regularized and accepted, was still in the eyes of the Church fornication. Men and women who lived in this relationship had to do so in the

102

knowledge that they were committing mortal sin and in danger of punishment by God. Furthermore, when a priest died, his widow was left without inheritance and his children without a name. As far as civil and canon law were concerned, the pastor's wife—no matter how faithful she had been to him—was only the priest's whore. She had no claims against the estate which she could prosecute and no position in society which she could occupy. On the other hand, fornication, while a mortal sin, was according to late medieval sexual morality a lesser crime against God than adultery (which violated the sacrament of marriage) or masturbation (which, as a crime against nature, was more heinous than rape). And so the practice of concubinage, if not condoned, was at least tolerated.

II

The Protestant Reformation constituted a sustained attack on the celibate ethic and a reemphasis on the dignity of the institution of marriage. Protestants did not deny that some men and women are called to a celibate life, though they regarded all claims to a celibate vocation with considerable suspicion, but they rejected the contention that celibacy should be made a law binding on all clergy. A vow in the very nature of the case destroys Christian freedom. While some Christians may be called to celibacy, all Christians are assuredly called to a life of freedom. Therefore celibacy which is received as a gift and is exercised in freedom may be celebrated as an authentic form of Christian discipleship. Celibacy which is made a law and enforced by a binding vow destroys the freedom that belongs to the essence of the Christian life and must therefore be rejected. Celibacy may be a charism; it may never be a law.

The distinction between commands and counsels was also rejected by Protestants, though not by all Protestants in exactly the same way. The Anabaptists, for example, concluded that non-resistance and pacifism were binding on all Christians, who were excluded by the teachings of Jesus in the Sermon on the Mount from all participation in public and political life. Luther, on the other hand, distinguished between what Christians were permitted to do in all matters that touched their own case exclusively (here the rigorous precepts of Jesus apply directly) and what they were obliged to do for the sake of their neighbor, who would be left at the mercy of sinful and rapacious men if they refused in such cases to resist evil forcibly. Christian love and responsibility even permit one to discharge the role of public executioner, though Christ forbids one to take revenge or to seek justice in a purely personal matter. But whether one followed Luther or the Anabaptists or any of the shades of Protestant opinion in between, all Protestants agreed that the distinction between commands and counsels was unacceptable in principle. The gifts and demands of the gospel are equally relevant for all Christians, clerical and lay. There is no heroic elite in the Church; or, perhaps one should say, all Christians are called to join that heroic elite. There is one standard of sanctity for all Christians.

No reason could be found by the Protestants for urging celibacy on their clergy. The pastor (only men were ordained in the sixteenth century) is not ontologically distinct from the laity. He has received no indelible character which communicates to him a sacramental power denied to the laity. The ministry of Word and sacrament belongs inherently to the common priesthood conferred on all Christians, male and female, in their baptism. Lay Christians exercise that ministry in private as they carry God's Word of judgment and grace to their neighbor. The pastor is ordained to preach that Word in public and preside at the Church's celebration of baptism and the eucharist. The distinction between clergy and layperson is primarily functional within the Body of Christ, though no one may exercise that function who has not been called to do so by God and acknowledged and confirmed in that office by some local congregation of believers. There is no reason, therefore, why the pastor, who differs from the laity only in function and vocation, should not marry and rear his own family. Indeed, the exercise of his vocation is helped rather than hindered by his family life and participation in ordinary social responsibilities.

Together with the rejection of celibacy as a law, the dissolution of the distinction between commands and counsels, and the stress on the functional character of the pastor's office, Protestants emphasized the interdependence of men and

105

women in a joint task of creating a Christian society. Marriage stands at the center of a God-given order. Matthew Zell, a Protestant preacher at the cathedral in Strassburg, argued in a famous sermon that, since woman was made from man, this proves not that women are subordinate to men but that men can only attain their full perfection in marriage. As Christ loved the Church, so men and women are to love one another and to seek their perfection in an interdependent relationship.

Just as marriage is the ordinary and proper state of life for the Protestant pastor, so, too, are women called to a more active role in the life and public ministry of the Church. Protestants did not advocate the ordination of women, though the stress on the common priesthood conferred in baptism and the redefinition of ordination in functional terms laid the foundation for the ordination of women in another place and time. Almost all of the arguments used today to defend the practice of the ordination of women were known in the sixteenth century, though none of the people who used them advocated such a radical break with the long-standing practice of the Christian churches. Nevertheless, the arguments were advanced, if only to support a more active role for women among the laity of the Church. When Katherine Zell, for example, was told by a critic that Paul told women to be silent in the Church, she responded that the same apostle had also taught that in Christ there is neither male nor female, bond nor free. Furthermore, the prophet Joel predicted that in the last days daughters as well as sons would prophesy. And no one who reads Luke's Gospel can fail to be impressed by the fact that Elizabeth was filled with the Holy Spirit while her husband, Zechariah, was struck dumb because of his unbelief. Women have a priesthood to discharge as well as men; like men they are to be Christ to the neighbor.

This Protestant teaching led to the initiation of certain social changes and sanctioned others, though one should be careful never to confuse the intention to effect a change with the change itself. One can, however, safely observe that the celibate ethic was utterly abandoned by Protestants, who nevertheless preserved the notion of an occasional charism of celibacy (which was forced to prove its credentials before a largely skeptical audience). Protestants turned the full force of their attention to the institution of marriage and emphasized the interdependence of men and women within it. Women were no longer regarded as simply dependent on their husbands, but were expected to assume an active role in their relationship to them. Martin Bucer once observed that the only defect of his second wife was that she did not criticize him. Mutual criticism is an expression of mutual love. Christians are called to seek their perfection in society rather than in isolation.

Protestant clergy, who were expected to marry (save in very rare and exceptional cases), were integrated more fully into society. The home and not the cloister became the arena for the exercise of the gentler Christian virtues. Marriage was not a concession to human weakness, but the chosen institution for the expression of the interdependence of male and female described in chapters one and two of Genesis. Not only the sexual act but the mutual society of male and female antedates the fall as the God-given purpose of marriage. "It is not good for man to be alone," was not spoken of human nature in a state of sin, but of man as male and female before the fall. Thus procreation and mutual society take precedence over the "remedy for concupiscence" as the principal purpose of marriage.

By rejecting the celibate ethic and emphasizing the institution of marriage as a means for the hallowing of human life, the Reformation created almost incidentally the office of pastor's wife. Women who had lived a shadowy existence as a priest's concubine were able to enter into a sexual relationship with their husbands within officially acknowledged bonds of matrimony. This was a gain not simply in the sense of delivering these women from an intolerable burden of guilt (which on Protestant grounds there was no conceivable reason for them to carry), but also in the sense of recognizing and honoring their inheritance rights as widows and the legitimacy of their children. It may be difficult for women who are currently seeking ordination to regard the creation of the pastor's wife as a great step forward in the liberation of women from unjust repression, but for the women involved the Reformation was a profoundly liberating event.

At the end of her life Katherine Zell described her role as a pastor's wife in Strassburg. While Katherine had no children and was able to assume far more duties in Church and community than the average laywoman, nevertheless she only claimed in practice a freedom accessible to other women in principle:

> That I learned to understand and helped to acknowledge the Gospel I shall let my God declare. That I married my pious husband and for this endured slander and lies, God knows. The work which I carried on both in the house and out is known both by those who already rest in God and those who are still living—how I helped to establish the Gospel, took in the exiled, comforted the homeless refugees, furthered the Church, preaching and the schools, God will remember even if the world may forget or did not notice . . . I honored, cherished and sheltered many great, learned men, with care, work, and expense . . . I listened to their conversation and their preaching, I read their books and their letters and they were glad to receive mine . . . and I must express how fond I was of all the old, great learned men and founders of the Church of Christ, how much I enjoyed listening to their talk of holy things and how my heart was joyful in these things.[3]

III

What can be concluded from this brief sketch as important for the Church in the present to consider? Let me note only some things that seem to me important:

1. The Protestant churches were correct to accept celibacy as a gift and to reject it as a law. Celibacy is an authentic form of Christian discipleship, and the freedom of the gospel means at the very least that some Christians, for whatever reasons, will be led to adopt this style of life. The

Protestant churches are in error, therefore, when they identify celibacy with homosexuality and make marriage a law. A church that respects the freedom of the gospel may not require its clergy to be celibate; by the same token a church that respects that same freedom dare not require its clergy to be married. Against such legalism stand the words of Jesus, the teaching of Luther, and the example of Paul and Asbury.

2. The Protestant emphasis on the interdependence of men and women in marriage and the common calling of men and women to seek the will of God in mutual relationship is an important corrective to theologies which subordinate women to men, on the one hand,[4] or which dispense with the relationship between male and female as trivial, on the other. Men and women are created for each other; they are bound to each other by ties of mutual dependence within the institution of marriage and outside it. The *imago dei* is an *imago trinitatis* in the sense that the society of Father, Son, and Holy Spirit is reflected in the society of man who is created male and female. Mutual dependence involves for most Christians the task of living a faithful covenant in sexual partnership. For Christians who choose celibacy it involves caring and sacrificial relationships with men and women in the full range of our common life together.

The plain fact is that Christian men and women need each other in order to be as much as possible the Church of Jesus Christ in our time and place, and to obey as fully as possible the will of God in our personal and corporate relationships. There is no room in the Church for misanthropy or misogyny. God who created us male and female calls us to perfection in mutual society. Christians who seek perfection in the exclusive society of one sex will not find it. Therefore while celibacy (which sublimates the sexual relationship between male and female) may be an authentic form of Christian discipleship, homosexuality (which denies that relationship) never is.

3. The Reformation did not sanction the ordination of women to the public ministry of Word and sacrament. Nevertheless, the fundamental arguments that sanction that act are already articulated in the Reformation era. Women share in the common priesthood committed to all the faithful by baptism. When women are ordained, they are only authorized to exercise in public a charism granted to them for private exercise by virtue of their incorporation into Christ. Women may be forbidden to preach and celebrate the eucharist only if it may be demonstrated that in Christ there is indeed male and female (contra Paul) and that in the last days sons shall prophesy while daughters shall demurely keep silent (contra Peter). Women already belong to a royal priesthood; otherwise they are not even members of the Church.

4. That a Christian is a female is no bar to valid ordination in the Church. But neither is it the basis on which ordination may be granted. Those persons—and only they—whether male or female, may be ordained for the public ministry of Word and sacrament who have been called to the ministry of God and who have demonstrated to the Church that they have—in the happy Wesleyan phrase—

"gifts, grace and the promise of usefulness." The office may be discharged by any baptized Christian, male or female; its discharge should be restricted, however, to those Christians who have been called to that ministry and whose vocation has been acknowledged by the Church. It is a scandal that women, who are rightly called to that office, are barred from it, while men, who are not, are admitted. Calling and not sex is the test of authentic ministry; the Church is called to prove the spirits, not determine the gender. It is difficult to avoid the conclusion that the arguments against the ordination of women, especially when they are combined with a laxity of standards with respect to the ordination of men, are only mere sophistry.

NOTES

1. Jacob Strauss, *Ein neuw wunderbarlich Beychtbeuchlin* (Augsburg, 1523) as quoted by Steven E. Ozment, *The Reformation in the Cities* (New Haven: Yale University Press, 1975), pp. 52-53.

2. Sebastian Brant, *The Ship of Fools,* trans. E. H. Zeydel (New York: Columbia University Press, 1941), p. 91.

3. Katherine Zell, *Ein Brief an die gentz Burgerschaft der Stadt Strassburg betreffend Hern Ludwig Rabus* (1557) as quoted by Miriam U. Chrisman, "Women and the Reformation in Strassburg 1490–1530," *Archive for Reformation History* 63 (1972), p. 157.

4. I do not mean to imply that traditional Protestant theology did not teach the subordination of women to men within the context of family and the home; it certainly did. But the emphasis on spiritual equality in Christ, a common priesthood, companionship as a fundamental purpose of marriage, and the rejection of celibacy stresses far more important motifs with historical consequences even within the sixteenth century itself. In his commentary on Genesis Calvin observed that the male was only half a man and that Adam saw himself complete in his wife. That is frequently overlooked in the rush to condemn Protestant teaching on the obedience of women to men. I cannot agree with the judgment of George Tavard that Protestantism has contributed little original insight to a theology of womanhood (cf. *Woman in Christian Tradition* [Notre Dame: University of Notre Dame Press, 1973], p. 171). It is Protestantism and not Eastern Orthodoxy or the Roman Catholic Church that has found a rationale for the ordination of women, not by rejecting its tradition, but by taking the implications of its tradition seriously.

SEVEN

Mary Reconsidered

Protestants are, on the whole, extremely reluctant to talk about Mary. If a Protestant theologian should dare to suggest that Mary's role in the history of salvation is an important theological issue, he would be informed that the matter is of concern to Roman Catholics and Eastern Orthodox Christians but scarcely to Protestants—as if what concerns two-thirds of Christendom could be of no significance to the remaining one-third! Even the early Fundamentalists who insisted on the Virgin Birth as one of the key fundamentals of the faith were less interested in Mary than in her virginity.

One can argue, of course, that the Protestant reluctance to talk about Mary reflects the New Testament's reluctance to offer much information about her. The Bible has really little to say about Mary and much of what it does say is not highly complimentary to her. She cannot seem to comprehend what her son is about and tries to interfere. Indeed, the blood relationship between

113

Jesus and Mary appears to stand in the way of her faith relationship. When a woman says to Jesus (Luke 11:27), "Blessed is the womb that bore you, and the breasts that you sucked," he responds, "Blessed rather are those who hear the word of God and keep it!" And when Jesus is notified (Mark 3:32) that "your mother and your brothers are outside, asking for you," he replies, "Whoever does the will of God is my brother, and sister, and mother." According to the witness of the New Testament, there is a distance between Jesus and his mother that can be bridged only by faith.

Luke's portrayal of Mary as humbly obedient when she learns she is to be mother of the Messiah and John's picture of her role at the cross are the high points of the New Testament witness to Mary. She is not at the center of the New Testament but at its periphery. At the time of the birth of Jesus and at the cross, Mary is not the initiator; she is the humble recipient and observer of the mysterious action of God. When Mary tries to intervene in the course of events, she is very much like Peter. She misunderstands what is happening and by her action stands in the way of the fulfillment of God's will.

But while the New Testament does not focus on Mary, it does have a number of impressive things to say about her. In the Gospel of Luke, Mary represents the remnant of Israel. When she breaks into song in the presence of her cousin Elizabeth, she sings the New Testament reformulation of the song of Hannah (I Sam. 2:4-7): "The feeble gird on strength. . . . Those who were hungry have ceased to hunger. The barren has borne seven. . . . The Lord . . . brings low, he also exalts."

The virginity of Mary is a sign of the divine initiative. As God brought forth a son from Sarah, who was too old to bear a child, so he brings forth a son from Mary, who as yet has no husband. In establishing the covenant with Abraham, God acted by creating a possibility where no human possibility existed. In fulfilling the covenant with Abraham, God once again created a new possibility for men and women where no natural possibility could be found. Sarah was the recipient of a covenantal blessing: "And God said to Abraham, 'As for Sarai your wife . . . I will bless her, and . . . she shall be a mother of nations; kings of peoples shall come from her' " (Gen. 17:15, 16). This covenantal blessing is echoed in the words of Luke 1:28, 42: "Hail, O favored one, the Lord is with you!" "Blessed are you among women, and blessed is the fruit of your womb!"[1] Mary is a sign of the continuity of the people of God, of Israel and the Church.

Of course, Protestants do not wholly neglect Mary. The Apostles' Creed confesses that Jesus was born of the Virgin Mary, and thus, by the back door, Mary enters into Protestant worship. There is little in the New Testament about the Virgin Birth itself. Matthew and Luke speak of it; possibly John also, though that is open to question. Paul makes no mention of it.

Contemporary men and women, who have difficulty believing in any kind of miraculous birth, stumble in the creed over the word "virgin." The ancient Church, though it knew as well as we how babies ordinarily come into existence, stumbled, not over "virgin" but over "born." The early Church proclaimed the good news that God had intervened in human history, that he had taken humanity upon himself, and become a man, though without surrendering his deity. The early Greeks to whom the gospel was declared found that improper. It was improper that an uncreated God should link himself with something created in this way. What could a transcendent God have to do with human clay? The word "born" as applied to God was a terrible stumbling block to the pagan mind of the early Christian world. Therefore the Virgin Mary was viewed as a sign that God had decisively intervened in human history for the redemption of sinners, that he had taken flesh in Jesus of Nazareth. The early Church was interested in Mary not for her own sake but only as a sign, a guarantee of the reality of the Incarnation. Although Mary is seen as the last of a covenantal line that begins with Sarah and is continued through Hannah and Elizabeth, affirmations about Mary are not about her but about her son. Mary is a signpost pointing to Jesus Christ and to the reality of the historical intervention of God in human history.

The unbiblical reluctance of Protestants to deal with the figure of Mary can be understood only as a reaction to certain later developments in the life of the Church. In the Middle Ages as well as in the earlier age of the Fathers, Mary increasingly became an object of interest in herself. I will attempt to summarize all the ways in which Mary claimed the attention of theologians, but only mention a few:

1. Immaculate conception. It is not really made clear in the New Testament why Mary should be the mother of Jesus Christ without the aid of a human father—unless, as John intimates in his description of regeneration as a kind of virgin birth, this marvelous act was intended to show that the advent of Jesus was not a human possibility but solely a divine one. Jesus was born, if one can apply the text of John 1:13 to Jesus rather than the Church, not by the will of man and not through man's cooperation but by the will of God alone.[2] And the sign for this is the virginity of Mary at the time of the birth of Jesus. Or perhaps, as Luke suggests, the Virgin Birth shows the extreme humility of Mary, who, precisely because she had no husband, occupied the bottom rung of Jewish society.

But this is speculation. The fact is, no theory is put forward to explain why Mary should be a virgin. Matthew stresses the idea that virgin birth fulfills the ancient prophecy of Isaiah 7:14, which only pushes the unanswered question further back in time; why was such a prophetic utterance made in the first place and why was it applied to Jesus? Luke feels that the Virgin Birth is further vindication of the principle that "with God nothing will be impossible," though the primary vindication of that principle is the conception of John the Baptist in the barren womb of his mother Elizabeth (Luke 1:37).

In the absence of any clear explanation for the necessity of the Virgin Birth, the Church began to devise theories. It connected procreation with lust and sin, and exalted virginity as a higher state of moral purity, as if a virgin could not be impure and as if procreation within marriage were not the will of God! Furthermore, the transmission of original sin was believed to take place in procreation, though the sexual act itself was not looked upon as evil. Lust is sinful, and fallen humanity conceives in lust. At the moment of conception, sin is mysteriously transmitted to the child by means of the perverted self-regard that accompanies the biological act. By doing away with birth through procreation, so the theory ran, Jesus was preserved from the human predicament in which we all find ourselves. He is not involved in original sin. Therefore he is Emmanuel and can save his people from their sins.

But what about Mary? Isn't it fitting for the mother of Jesus also to be preserved from original sin? Wouldn't that contribute to the guarantee that her son could not be involved in hereditary sinfulness? If there is no sinful procreation and if the mother herself is preserved from original sin, then surely the Savior is free from all taint of sin.

The Catholic Church did not, of course, affirm that Mary was also born of a virgin (since there was no biblical evidence to support such a theory), but rather that she was sanctified and preserved from sin through an immaculate conception. When some theologians (such as Thomas Aquinas) argued that to exempt Mary from sin would undercut the centrality of Jesus Christ as Redeemer,[3] they were told (by Duns Scotus, among others) that one gives greater honor to Jesus Christ by saying

118

that he preserved the Virgin Mary from sin than by holding that he waited to save her only after she had fallen.

2. *The maternity of Mary.* Mary is not simply a virgin; she is also a mother. And the medieval Church rang the changes on that theme. God chose Mary to be the mother of Jesus Christ, as he once chose Abraham to be the father of his people, Israel. According to the Genesis account, when God made man he took the dust of the earth. But redemption begins, not with dust, but with the body of Mary. It is from her flesh that the Messiah comes. Mary is the second Eve, the fulfillment of Genesis 3:15.

God chose Mary. But Mary, according to medieval Catholic thought, merited that choice. She cooperates with God in becoming the mother of Jesus Christ. God does not use her as a potter uses clay or as he once used the dust of the earth from which he formed Adam. Mary has freedom of choice. She chooses to cooperate with God; she accepts the message of the angel in Luke's narrative; she gives her assent. That choice, that assent, that cooperation, is meritorious.

Mary is thus a type of the Church. Like Mary, the Church has freedom of choice, the ability to decide. God respects the human reality of the Church. He does not deal with it as if it were inert clay. And the Church's choice to cooperate with God is meritorious. God respects the creation he has made. He deals with it as a responsible covenant partner. And he graciously rewards the good works of that partner. God does not destroy human freedom but works with that freedom.

119

Mary is also an example for the Church. She obediently and humbly accepted the role God offered her, even though it brought her suffering. There is no obedience to God that does not involve some personal cost to oneself. The Church is called to imitate Mary, her obedience and selfless love.

3. *Cooperation in redemption.* Now we come to a crucial point, that of Mary's cooperation in redemption. Mary is more than mother and virgin; she is also a covenant partner. At the cross Mary does not stand above or below her son; she stands beside him, sharing in his sorrows and suffering as only a mother can suffer. But for the good of the Church and its redemption, Mary takes the suffering of her son upon herself. She offers him to God the Father for the sake of the Church, even at the cost of her own spiritual torment. At the cross she is the bride of Christ. Through the sufferings of Mary and her son, the Church is born. Jesus came from Mary's womb, but the Church comes from her broken heart. All forsake Jesus and flee, all except Mary. She belongs to the faithful remnant of God's covenant people. It is not the case that all humanity has been faithless to God and that God finds a faithful covenant partner only in Jesus Christ. Mary, too, is faithful. She is the elect remnant. And from her faithfulness and the faithfulness of Jesus Christ, the redemption of the world is effected. As Mary consents to the Incarnation, so she consents to the cross, and by her consent and self-sacrifice she cooperates in the work of redemption.

At this juncture one must not forget the analogy

120

between Mary and the Church. The Church, like Mary, is also the mother of the faithful. A Christian is born in the womb of the Church, nourished by its sacraments and teaching. Like Mary the Church also stands by a cross, not the cross on Calvary but the cross over the altar. Like Mary the Church offers Christ to the Father, in this case as a re-presentation of the body and blood of Christ for the sins of the people in the unbloody sacrifice of the mass.

4. Intercessor. Mary is not only mother, virgin, and bride. She is also intercessor.[4] In the Middle Ages it became increasingly difficult for ordinary Christians to believe that Jesus Christ was really a man. People tended to think of him solely as divine. Consequently, he receded farther and farther into heaven, and became more and more remote and inaccessible. Increasingly, it was Mary to whom people looked for compassion. Jesus Christ was a judge who spent his time scrutinizing Christians to make sure that they were using to best advantage the means of grace he had provided for them in the Church and the sacraments.

A second development was closely related to this. Jesus Christ was the God-man. He was perfectly obedient to the will of God. But in this obedience he had an advantage over ordinary men and women. He could be obedient in the power of his divine nature. We do not have this advantage. When we are tempted, we have no divine nature to give us the power to obey. How can Jesus, therefore, really understand the temptations that befall ordinary men and women? How can he have compassion on

121

them? Mary on the other hand is wholly human. Originally to call Mary pure was simply to call attention to her freedom from the taint of sin. But this began to take on a new meaning. To call Mary a pure human being was to call her a *real* human being. She obeyed and pleased God without a divine nature. As a real human being Mary can have pity on us in our sins and temptations. One should therefore pray to the compassionate Mary; she will pray to her son; and her son cannot really deny his mother's requests.

The medieval vision of the role of Mary is a vision that Protestants cannot affirm. Mary as one who cooperates with God or who participates in the redemption of the world is a theological point of view that Protestants reject. Human beings do not cooperate with God in the sense of earning merits. Good works are given, not to God, who does not need them, but to the neighbor, who clearly does. Any view in which Mary or the Church offers something to God reverses the direction of both the original sacrifice of Jesus and the eucharistic sacrifice. We do not offer a sacrifice to God to procure his benefits; the movement is all the other way. God offers himself to us in the suffering love of the cross. God nourishes the Church through the benefits of Word and sacrament. We do not offer anything to God, except perhaps gratitude and praise. God offers everything to us, which we then gladly share with our neighbor. Mary as co-worker and Mary as co-offerer are images that Protestants cannot accept.

Moreover, Protestants agree with Thomas

Aquinas in opposing any Marian theology that undercuts the centrality of Jesus Christ. God found a faithful covenant partner only in his son. Since Mary is a mythical personification of the Church, there is a very real danger, as Gerhard Ebeling has pointed out, that a church that glorifies the fidelity of Mary and her role in the redemption of the world is a church that glorifies itself.

1. On the other hand, Mary is a sign that God has really intervened in human history, really involved himself in our human clay, our suffering, our temptations. If there is a reason to reject a theology that is interested in Mary in herself, there is no reason to reject one that makes affirmations about Mary as a signpost pointing away from herself to God's mysterious activity in Jesus Christ. Mary is humble. She stands at the periphery of the New Testament; and there is where she should be. She is a sign pointing to Jesus Christ. Truly biblical Mariology is only another term for Christology.

2. Mary is also a sign that God's new act in Christ stands in historic continuity with his saving acts in the Old Testament. To be sure, Christian theologians are correct when they say that the Messiah undercuts many of the expectations of the Old Testament. In a very real sense the Messiah who comes is not the Messiah who is expected. But Mary is a sign that the promise is fulfilled as well as transformed. With Simeon, Anna, Zechariah, Elizabeth, and John the Baptist, Mary belongs to the Old Testament people of God who stand on the threshold of fulfillment. A church that takes Mary seriously may say no not only to denials of Christ's

humanity but also to denials of the authority of the Old Testament.

3. Furthermore, the image of Mary as a type or analogue of the Church is not a bad one, so long as the whole biblical witness is taken. Mary is not only the obedient maiden, she is not only the sorrowing mother; she is also one who does not understand what God's purposes are, who intervenes when she ought to keep silent, who interferes and tries to thwart the purpose of God, who pleads the ties of filial affection when she should learn faith. And that is what the Church is like. It is not only faithful; it is faithless. It is not only a custodian of God's truth; it falsifies the Word of God as well. The Church like Mary is just and sinful alike, obedient and interfering, perceptive and opaque, faithful and faithless. It is false theology to say that Mary, because she is feminine, adds an element of compassion that is somehow missing in God. On the contrary, there are no bounds to the compassion of God, of which the compassion of Mary is a finite and limited reflection. Like the rest of the Church, Mary loves because she was first beloved.

Mary confesses that she is not worthy to be chosen by God. That is not false humility. It is the truth of every human being's situation before God. The words of Luther on his deathbed are applicable to Mary as well as to the Church of which she is the type: "We are beggars; this is true." To recognize this fact is to give Mary her true honor, to recognize her rightful place in the history of salvation. Mary is the sign of the continuity and reality of God's saving activity. To understand this is to hear in the salutation the echo of the blessing of Sarah; to find in her song the strains of Hannah's; to say with Luke: "Hail, O favored one, the Lord is with you! . . . Blessed are you among women, and blessed is the fruit of your womb!"

NOTES

1. The addition of the phrase "Mother of God" to the *Ave Maria* grows out of the Nestorian controversy of the fifth century. The Orthodox Fathers ascribed to Mary, the mother of Jesus, the title of *Theotokos* or God-bearer, which better preserved the Word-flesh Christology of Alexandria against the Word-man Christology of Antioch. Curiously, the West did not use the exact Latin equivalent, *Deipara,* but rather the phrase *Dei Genetrix* or Mother of God. The intention, however, was the same: to preserve the high Christology of Chalcedon rather than to ascribe special honor to Mary herself. The later medieval theologians saw in Mary's role as *Theotokos* the basis of her work as intercessor.

2. The suggestion that John 1:13 is an indirect allusion to the Virgin Birth was first made by Hans von Campenhausen in his book *Die Jungfrauengeburt in der Theologie der alten Kirche,* Sitzungsberichte der Heidelberger Akadamie der Wissenschaften, Phil. hist. Klasse, Abh. 3 (1962), p. 12.

3. Because of the opposition of Thomas Aquinas and the Dominicans to the doctrine of the immaculate conception, it was not promulgated as a dogma until the Council of Basel (1439). Since it was proferred in a session that was not confirmed, the teaching did not become official dogma of the Roman Catholic Church until restated by Pius IX in 1854 in the papal bull *Ineffabilis Deus.* Martin Luther and Huldrych Zwingli were raised in a late medieval tradition that supported the doctrine of the immaculate conception.

4. The doctrine of the bodily assumption of Mary into heaven did not gain official status as a dogma until 1950, when it was promulgated by Pius XII in the bull *Munificentissimus Deus.* The bodily assumption did have vigorous support among certain theologians in the late Middle Ages. Gabriel Biel (d. 1495), for example, tied the doctrine of the bodily assumption to the role of Mary as intercessor. He did not, however, believe that faith in the bodily assumption of Mary was necessary to salvation. The contention that belief in the assumption is necessary to salvation is a modern problem.

EIGHT

Inclusive Language
and the Trinity

Some Christians have become concerned about the use of inclusive language in public worship. The traditional reference to God as Father, Son, and Holy Spirit with its strongly patriarchal overtones has troubled Christians who feel that more neutral language should be used in the Church's confessions and acts of public worship. Various solutions and remedies have been suggested. One of the less radical proposals is embodied in a new version of the "Gloria Patri," which has been adopted by some congregations. The words run as follows:

> Glory be to our Creator,
> Praise to our Redeemer, Lord,
> Glory be to our Sustainer,
> Ever three and ever one,
> As it was in the beginning,
> Ever shall be, amen.

On the face of it, there seems to be nothing objectionable in this formulation. It is certainly appropriate in every generation for Christians to praise the activity of God as Creator, Redeemer, and Sustainer. It is also appropriate for Christian congregations to try to find ways to use inclusive language in worship as long as the substance of the Christian faith can be preserved. Women have suffered from discrimination and repression in Western culture, not least at the hands of Christian churches. The use of more inclusive language is one way the Church can repent of its sins and begin to lead a godly, righteous, and holy life.

The difficulty with this "Gloria" is that it is put forward as a trinitarian confession ("ever three and ever one"), when it is nothing of the kind. The doctrine of the Trinity is not merely the teaching that God is three in his historical self-revelation to us, while remaining one God, but that in the mystery of the unity of his inner life God is three to himself as well. It is an affirmation of the nature of unconditioned reality and not merely about the nature of revelation. Trinity is, like predestination, a doctrine that does not make complete sense in itself but does make luminous sense of other things.

Creator, Redeemer, and Sustainer refer to historical operations of God. To affirm that one God acted in these three roles is at best sub-trinitarian and at worst a repetition of the old Sabellian heresy. Furthermore, if Creator is looked upon as an exact replacement for Father, Redeemer for Son, and Sustainer for Holy Spirit, then both too much and too little is claimed for each person of the Trinity. If the Father is only Creator and not Redeemer and Sustainer, if the Son is only

127

Redeemer and not Creator and Sustainer, if the Holy Spirit is only Sustainer and not Creator and Redeemer, then the Bible becomes unintelligible. What does John mean when he speaks of the Logos as the one through whom all things were made? What does Isaiah mean when he celebrates Yahweh as Redeemer? What does the Church have in mind when it prays, "Veni Creator Spiritus"? You can see rather quickly why the Church adopted the theological principle that the works of God *ad extra,* i.e., directed outside himself, are indivisible.

The last phrase, "as it was in the beginning, ever shall be, amen," is also confusing if it is posited of the historical operations of God. Do the authors of the revised "Gloria" intend to confess that God is eternally Creator? If so, do they intend to affirm the eternity of creation as an indispensable companion of God, along the lines discussed by Tertullian in his controversy with Hermogenes? It is difficult to tell just what is meant when language whose reference is temporal is substituted for language whose reference is supra-historical. Very probably the intention is to save the trinitarian formulation, while removing nothing more than the offending non-inclusive language. Unfortunately, the results do not match the good intentions. It is clear, in other words, if we are going to revise our language of worship, we have to pick up the debate where it left off and not proceed as though such a debate never took place.

What I propose to do in this essay is to take a look at the doctrine of the Trinity in historical perspective. Why did the Church confess that God is both one and three and what theological purposes did this doctrine serve? Obviously, I cannot hope in such a brief article to say everything that could be said about this subject, but I want to suggest several main themes that need to be considered in any further debate about this issue.

I

The doctrine of the Trinity is not a biblical doctrine in the sense that it is directly taught in the New Testament. What one finds in the New Testament is the apostolic preaching of a God revealed as Father, Son, and Holy Spirit, together with the ancient confession of Israel that God is one. The doctrine of the Trinity is a product of the Church's reflection on its own proclamation. How can it confess that God is one without obscuring or confusing the threeness of God's self-revelation? How can it confess that God is three without lapsing into polytheism? In accounting for its own proclamation and in avoiding the twin dangers of unitarianism and polytheism, the Church found that the doctrine of the Trinity clarified not only the Church's understanding of God but a number of other doctrinal problems as well.

Take, for example, the problem of the intelligibility of the Bible. Fairly early on, heretical movements in the Church attempted to offer alternative readings of the Bible that interpreted salvation as a rescue of divine fragments embedded in the soul from the world of matter or that pitted the Redeemer God of the New Testament against the Creator God of the Old. These alternative readings were opposed by Irenaeus and Tertullian, among others, who argued that the mere possession of a violin did not make one a violinist. To understand the Bible correctly, one must understand its underlying structure.[1]

These theologians had in mind certain clever people in the late Roman world who liked to compose poems by taking lines from established poets and combining them in a new way. They would take lines, say, from the first, fourth, and fifth books of Virgil's *Aeneid,* add a few lines from his *Eclogues,* and create a new poem. If one were to ask whether every line in the poem had been written by Virgil, the answer would be yes. Not a single verse in the poem had been composed by the anonymous "poet"; every word was authentic Virgil. But if one were to ask whether Virgil had written the poem, the answer would be a resounding no. Every line was from Virgil, yet Virgil had not written the poem. What had changed was the underlying pattern, the architectonic structure of the whole.

Irenaeus and Tertullian compared the heretics to these clever drawing-room poets. Every word they cite in their writings is from the Bible, yet their teaching is not biblical. What has changed is the underlying pattern, the unifying structural principle, the *skopos* of the whole. Only if the Bible is cited and interpreted in accordance with its underlying structure, will it speak once again with the authentic voice of the prophets and apostles.

130

What is the underlying pattern of the Bible? It is summarized in the expanded baptismal confession: "I believe in God the Father Almighty, maker of heaven and earth; and in Jesus Christ his only Son our Lord . . . [and] in the Holy Spirit." This confession is regarded as both the underlying structure of the whole Bible and the purest distillate of its teaching. The Bible is about God, Father, Son, and Holy Spirit. Not to interpret it from that perspective is to misinterpret it.

How can the Church be certain that it has the right hermeneutical key to the Bible, that it is interpreting the Bible from the right perspective? Irenaeus answers that question by referring to lists of bishops the Church has preserved to validate its teaching. The bishops in the present who teach their flocks to read the Bible as the self-revelation of God under the three names were taught by bishops who were in turn taught by the apostles themselves. Only two generations separated Irenaeus from Christ. The Church, therefore, is not only the inheritor of documents from the apostolic age; it is the beneficiary of a living teaching tradition initiated by the apostles.

The conviction that the Bible was to be read in this way left the Church face to face with the real trinitarian problem: How were the three names to be reconciled with the confession that God is one? A number of solutions were proposed and found wanting.

The Arians in the fourth century proposed to reconcile the names of God with traditional monotheism by arguing that the Son is metaphysically inferior to the Father, a divine being, to be sure, but not God in the same sense that the Father is God. The Son is the first creature of God, superior to all other creatures and the agent of their creation, but still subordinate to the Father from whom he derives. Objections to this view took many forms, not the least of which was the complaint that Arian religion did not adequately account for the biblical texts that ascribe deity to the Son. The Arians lost themselves in details of biblical exegesis but failed to provide an explanation large enough to account for all the biblical data.

Sabellius in the third century provided a rival explanation. He conceded that the Son was fully God but looked upon the names, Father, Son, and Spirit, as attributes rather than as persons. Or to put that differently, he argued that God played many roles in history and that the three names were masks that God wore in the performance of those roles. Like Sir Alec Guinness, who played an entire family in the 1949 British movie, *Kind Hearts and Coronets,* God is capable of assuming different guises at different times in the course of his self-manifestation in history.

This view also created exegetical difficulties. The story of the baptism of Jesus forms a case in point. According to the Evangelist, when Jesus is baptized, the Father says that Jesus is his well-beloved Son, and the Spirit descends on him like a dove (Mark 1:9-11). While Sabellians can explain how God can play different roles at different times, they cannot explain how God can play three different roles at the same time. Nor can they account for the prayer life of Jesus, at least for his last agonizing prayers in Gethsemane and on the cross. Unless there are real relations between the Father and the Son and not merely imaginary relations, the prayers of Jesus seem a curious charade.

Problems such as these led the Church to conclude that the Bible is unintelligible unless God is not only three to us but also three to himself. While there is one God, that God exists in society. Such society is reflected in the historical self-revelation of God and his activity as Father, Son, and Spirit, but is not exhausted by it. Trinity is not merely a doctrine of how God acts; it is a doctrine of who and what God is. Therefore is can only be described by language appropriate to the verb "is"; namely, the language of being.

The appropriation by the Church of metaphysical language about God does not represent a Hellenistic corruption of the simple Hebraic gospel of Jesus and his love. The New Testament itself with its proclamation of one God under the three names compels the Church to speak metaphysically of God. One has only to read the accounts of the baptism of Jesus (Mark 1:9-11; Matt. 3:16-17; Luke 3:21-22), the language of the great commission (Matt. 28:19; Acts 1:7-8), the last discourse of Christ with his disciples (John 15:1-27; 16:1-15), or the Pauline and deutero–Pauline references to the work of the Spirit, Christ, and God (Rom. 8:9-11; I Cor. 12:4-6; II Cor. 13:14; Gal. 4:4-7; II Thess. 2:13-14; Eph. 4:4-6) to realize how swiftly one is forced by the text to confront questions about the being as well as the activity of God. Without the

133

ontological Trinity, the Church cannot adequately account for such texts. The Church is obliged to confess the Trinity because it is committed to the public interpretation of the Bible.

II

The doctrine of the Trinity has also had an immediate bearing on the Church's understanding of the sacraments and their role in human salvation. That bearing is obvious in the case of baptism, since Christians are baptized in the name of the Father, Son, and Holy Spirit. It is less obvious, but no less important in the case of the eucharist. The early opponents of the Arians saw this point and pressed it hard.

To understand the Greek insistence that the doctrine of the Trinity is practical because it touches on the central acts of worship of the Christian community, one must bear in mind the understanding of the drama of redemption embraced by the fourth-century theologians. We Western Christians tend to think of redemption as primarily a matter of sin and forgiveness. Human beings have sinned against God and other human beings and need to be pardoned. Greek Christians, on the other hand, tended to think of redemption primarily as victory over death and human mortality.

As the Greeks saw it, the principal human predicament from which there is no escape is the brutal fact of death. Death is not a gentle release from the world of materiality in which we have been imprisoned, but the last great enemy that threatens to thwart the purposes of God and to deprive human existence of all meaning. We are branches on a dying tree called Adam, whose roots have been cut even through its trunk is still sending out fresh shoots. But the signs of life are deceptive; the fresh shoots are, to use the phrase of Dylan Thomas, "green and dying." Cut off from the source of life, the whole human race is given over to death.

Only God is his own autonomous and endless source of life. It is therefore necessary for the branches to be cut off from the dying tree called Adam and transplanted in God, the endless source of inexhaustible life. But how can such a transplantation take place? It is here that the doctrines of Trinity and Incarnation become crucial.

The dying branches of Adam are cut off by baptism and transplanted into Christ. Because Christ is the Son and therefore fully God, he can serve as the source of life for human beings united to him by faith and baptism. Because Christ is the offspring of Mary and therefore fully human, it is possible for human beings to be so united to him. If he were not human, such a union would be impossible. If he were not God, such a union would be pointless.

The eucharist is the sacrament through which this union is nurtured and perfected. Through the eucharist the Son is present in his divine (the doctrine of the Trinity) and human natures (the doctrine of the Incarnation). As baptism and faith communicated life to the human soul, so, too, the eucharist by a kind of reverse metabolism communicates life to

135

the human body. Other food is digested by Christian believers, but the eucharist as a heavenly food digests its own communicants, making them immortal and giving them a share in resurrection life.

All of this realistic language is used to combat views of the sonship of Christ which can be accommodated to a moralistic view of human salvation. Adoptionists taught, for example, that Jesus was a human being who merited adoption as a Son of God by his exemplary moral behavior. The implication of this view was that ordinary human beings could merit becoming sons and daughters of God by imitating the life of Jesus and conforming their behavior to his. Recent research has uncovered a similar mind-set among the Arians.

The doctrine of the Trinity is articulated in opposition to the myth that human beings can redeem themselves by exemplary moral conduct or that the initiative for human redemption comes from below. The story of Jesus is not the story of a human being who achieves elevation to sonship by his meritorious obedience to the will of God, but of a divine Son who condescends to assume human flesh in order to set right a situation that could have been corrected in no other way. What is at stake in the doctrine of the Trinity is not merely an understanding of the nature of God, but a vision of the nature of human salvation.

III

Augustine attempted to make the doctrine of the Trinity rationally comprehensible by drawing on analogies from human experience. Just as a human being has understanding, memory, and will without ceasing to be a single human personality, so, too, God is Father, Son, and Spirit without ceasing to be one God. In fact, argued Augustine, one would expect human nature to reflect a certain threefoldness-in-unity, since human beings were made in the image of a triune God. The image of God is by definition an image of the Trinity.

Probably the most important analogy that Augustine drew was an analogy between the inner life of God and the act of love. The act of loving requires for its completion a lover, a beloved, and the bond of love. In the inner life of the Trinity, the Father is the Lover, the Son is the Beloved, and the Holy Spirit is the mutual bond of Love that binds them. The use of this analogy had an important consequence for Christian discourse about God.

It offered one of the clearest explanations ever conceived of the aseity of God; i.e., of the independence of God from creation and of the perfection of God's life apart from it. Just as lovers need nothing but each other and the love that binds them, so God was complete in himself prior to creation, requiring nothing outside himself for his perfection. If that is true, then both creation and redemption are graces, unmerited gifts of God, who needed neither to create nor to redeem. While God cannot will his own non-existence and cannot exist otherwise than as a Trinity (since that is a matter of nature and not of will), God has an absolute right to create nothing outside himself.

It was precisely this point that the Greek

theologian Origen was unwilling to grant. Since God is eternal and immutable, God must always have been what he is now. Since God is now known as Creator, he must always have been Creator. The idea of a God who was inactive and not therefore eternally creating was absurd to Origen. If God is an eternal Creator, then the world is an eternal companion of God. To affirm the opposite is to affirm a potential in the being of God that has never been actualized. A contingent world implies a mutable God. Origen sees no other possible conclusion.

Athanasius recognized that Origen had failed to separate the problem of the generation of the Son by the Father from the problem of the creation of the world.[2] The absolute being of God and the contingent being of the world are two radically dissimilar modes of existence. The relationship between Father and Son is eternal and necessary; the relationship between God and the world is contingent and voluntary. The mystery of God is that he cannot not exist; the mystery of creation is that it need not have existed at all.

In the movie *Tin Men,* one of the salesman tells another that he was recently impressed at a salad bar by the sudden realization of the probable existence of God. "All those vegetables," he says, "coming out of the earth—and I hadn't even gotten to the fruits." This exchange leads to one of the great comic scenes in the movie in which the salesman to whom he has spoken prays in front of a salad bar like a priest at an altar. While all of this is proposed in great good fun and without any intention of being serious, the screen writer has actually touched on a central theme of trinitarian theology: the richness and diversity of creation as an illustration of the goodness of God who created as a gift for others what he did not need for himself.

That insight is lost if we focus on the historical activity of God as Creator and dismiss all talk of an ontological Trinity. It is, of course, a good thing to confess that God is Creator; it is even better to confess with Augustine the aseity of God, who made the cosmos for the sheer joy of giving it to others. Nothing in the world is there by necessity; everything is there by choice. Nothing in the world exists because God could not live without it; everything—at least everything good—exists as a gift. I cannot properly enjoy an ear of corn or a walk in the cool evening breezes or conversation with old friends, unless and until I know that it is the personal gift of a good God, who gave to me what he was under no compulsion to give. The Christian confession of one God eternally subsisting in three persons is a confession of the gratuitous goodness of all good things.

IV

This brief survey of trinitarian theology has given us, I think, some guidelines by which to test inclusive language reformulations of the doctrine of the Trinity. Does the new language account in a more comprehensive or penetrating way for the biblical data than did the old language? Does it offer a vision of salvation compatible with Christian tradition? Does it protect the transcendence of God and the goodness of the created order? If it does, it ought to be gladly embraced by all. If it does not, it ought to be rejected.

I have already indicated why I feel that the triad, Creator, Redeemer, Sustainer, will not do as a substitute for the older language of Father, Son, and Holy Spirit. That does not mean that such language cannot be used in Christian worship, but only that it cannot be used in such a way as to give the impression that it is trinitarian language. Not all names of God are trinitarian names; some are names of operations. Creator, Redeemer, Sustainer are operational or economic names. But trinitarian language is ontological language. It is the language of God's being and not of God's doing.

As the language of God's being, it is more primitive, more foundational, more inescapable than the language of God's doing. God was Father before he was Creator (I am speaking logically rather than temporally). He would have been Father even if he had never created. Father represents God's relationship to God and only in a later and subordinate sense God's relationship to creatures. Creator never represents God's relationship to God, but solely God's relationship to creatures. God is Father by nature and Creator by choice.

The commitment of the Church to the ontological Trinity does not forbid it from using other names in the liturgy, such as the Good Shepherd, the True Vine, the Bread from Heaven, or even

140

the Mother from whom we have been born and by whom we are comforted (Deut. 32:11; Ps. 131:2; Job 38:29; Isa. 42:14; 49:14-15; 66:13; Matt. 23:37; Luke 15:8-10; John 1:13; 3:5-8). Since there are no Christians by natural birth but only by conversion, and since "born-again" Christian is a tautology, the Johannine image of the Holy Spirit as the Mother who brings us to spiritual birth is a metaphor that ought to have played more of a role in Christian worship than it has. However, what is not permitted to the Church is to abandon the use of trinitarian language for God or to substitute other names for the ontological names of Father, Son, and Spirit. To keep silence in a time of conflict over the doctrine of the Trinity is to commit what Karl Rahner calls "virtual heresy." To baptize or ordain in the economic names of Creator, Redeemer, and Sustainer, is to leave catholic Christianity for an enthusiastic sect.

Someone may object that no human language can capture the reality of God. That is, of course, true. The mystery of God always exceeds our intellectual grasp. God is beyond sexuality, beyond male and female, and the names of God have an analogical rather than a univocal signification. Christian theology has always insisted that apophatic theology, which proceeds by denial of what God is not, is higher than kataphatic theology, which proceeds by affirmation.

The implied counter-proposition, however, is not true; namely, that because our affirmations cannot capture the mystery of God's being, it does not matter very much what we call God. I have

141

spent a good deal of time in this essay trying to show exactly how much was at stake in the use of trinitarian language by the Church. Trinitarian theology influenced how Christians interpreted the Bible, how they understood the drama of redemption and their role in it, even how they valued the created world around them. Other, more inclusive, ways of talking about God may serve to achieve the same ends, though the burden of proof in this as in all reconsiderations of Christian tradition rests on the aspiring Reformers.

NOTES

1. In this connection, see the illuminating discussion by Georges Florovsky, "The Function of Tradition in the Ancient Church," in *Bible, Church, Tradition: An Eastern Orthodox View* (Belmont, Mass.: Nordland Publishing Company, 1972), pp. 73-92; and "The Authority of the Ancient Councils and the Tradition of the Fathers," pp. 93-103.

2. On the doctrine of creation, see Georges Florovsky, "St. Athanasius' Concept of Creation," in *Aspects of Church History* (Belmont, Mass.: Nordland Publishing Company, 1975), pp. 39-62.

NINE

The Superiority of
Pre-Critical Exegesis

In 1859 Benjamin Jowett, then Regius Professor of Greek in the University of Oxford, published a justly famous essay on the interpretation of Scripture.[1] Jowett argued that "Scripture has one meaning—the meaning which it had in the mind of the Prophet or Evangelist who first uttered or wrote, to the hearers or readers who first received it."[2] Scripture should be interpreted like any other book and the later accretions and venerated traditions surrounding its interpretation should, for the most part, either be brushed aside or severely discounted. "The true use of interpretation is to get rid of interpretation, and leave us alone in company with the author."[3]

Jowett did not foresee great difficulties in the way of the recovery of the original meaning of the text. Proper interpretation requires imagination, the ability to put oneself into an alien cultural situation, and knowledge of the language and history of the ancient people whose literature one sets out to interpret. In the case of the Bible, one has also to bear in mind the progressive nature of revelation and the superiority of certain later religious insights to certain earlier ones. But the interpreter, armed with the proper linguistic tools, will find that "universal truth easily breaks through the accidents of time and place"[4] and that such truth still speaks to the condition of the unchanging human heart.

Of course, critical biblical studies have made enormous strides since the time of Jowett. No reputable biblical scholar would agree today with Jowett's reconstruction of the Gospels in which Jesus appears as a "teacher . . . speaking to a group of serious, but not highly educated, working men, attempting to inculcate in them a loftier and sweeter morality."[5] Still, the quarrel between modern biblical scholarship and Benjamin Jowett is less a quarrel over hermeneutical theory than it is a disagreement with him over the application of that theory in his exegetical practice. Biblical scholarship still hopes to recover the original intention of the author of a biblical text and still regards the pre-critical exegetical tradition as an obstacle to the proper understanding of the true meaning of that text. The most primitive meaning of the text is its only valid meaning, and the historical-critical method is the only key that can unlock it.

But is that theory true?

I think it is demonstrably false. In what follows I want to examine the pre-critical exegetical tradition at exactly the point at which Jowett regarded it to be most vulnerable, namely, in its refusal to bind the meaning of any pericope to the intention, whether explicit or merely half-formed, of its human author. Medieval theologians defended the proposition, so alien to modern biblical studies, that the meaning of Scripture in the mind of the prophet who first uttered it is only one of its possible meanings and may not, in certain circum- stances, even be its primary or most important meaning. I want to show that this theory (in at least that respect) was superior to the theories that replaced it. When biblical scholarship shifted from the hermeneutical position of Origen to the hermeneutical position of Jowett, it gained some- thing important and valuable. But it lost something as well, and it is the painful duty of critical scholarship to assess its losses as well as its gains.

I

Medieval hermeneutical theory took as its point of departure the words of Paul: "The letter kills, but the Spirit gives life" (II Cor. 3:6, NIV). Augustine suggested that this text could be understood in either one of two ways. On the one hand, the distinction between letter and Spirit could be a distinction between law and gospel, between demand and grace. The letter kills because it demands an obedience of the sinner that the sinner is powerless to render. The Spirit makes alive because it infuses the forgiven sinner with new power to meet the rigorous requirements of the law.

But Paul could also have in mind a distinction between what William Tyndale later called the "story-book" or narrative level of the Bible and the deeper theological meaning or spiritual significance implicit within it. This distinction was important for at least three reasons. Origen stated the first reason with unforgettable clarity:

> Now what man of intelligence will believe that the first and the second and the third day, and the evening and the morning existed without the sun and moon and stars? And that the first day, if we may so call it, was even without a heaven? And who is so silly as to believe that God, after the manner of a farmer, "planted a paradise eastward in Eden," and set in it a visible and palpable "tree of life," of such a sort that anyone who tasted its fruit with his bodily teeth would gain life; and again that one could partake of "good and evil" by masticating the fruit taken from the tree of that name? And when God is said to "walk in the paradise in the cool of the day" and Adam to hide himself behind a tree, I do not think anyone will doubt that these are figurative expressions which indicate certain mysteries through a semblance of history and not through actual events.[6]

Simply because a story purports to be a straightforward historical narrative does not mean that it is in fact what it claims to be. What appears to be history may be metaphor or figure instead and the interpreter who confuses metaphor with literal fact is an interpreter who is simply incompetent. Every biblical story means something, even if the narrative taken at face value contains absurdities or contradictions. The interpreter must demythologize the text in order to grasp the sacred mystery cloaked in the language of actual events.

The second reason for distinguishing between letter and spirit was the thorny question of the relationship between Israel and the Church, between the Greek Testament and the Hebrew Bible. The Church regarded itself as both continuous and discontinuous with ancient Israel. Because it claimed to be continuous, it felt an unavoidable obligation to interpret the Torah, the Prophets and the Writings. But it was precisely this claim of continuity, absolutely essential to Christian identity, that created fresh hermeneutical problems for the Church.

How was a French parish priest in 1150 to understand Psalm 137, which bemoans captivity in Babylon, makes rude remarks about Edomites, expresses an ineradicable longing for a glimpse of Jerusalem, and pronounces a blessing on anyone who avenges the destruction of the temple by dashing Babylonian children against a rock? The priest lives in Concale, not Babylon, has no personal quarrel with Edomites, cherishes no ambitions to visit Jerusalem (though he might fancy a holiday in Paris), and is expressly forbidden by Jesus to avenge himself on his enemies. Unless Psalm 137 has more than one possible meaning, it cannot be used as a prayer by the Church and must be rejected as a lament belonging exclusively to the piety of ancient Israel.

A third reason for distinguishing letter from Spirit was the conviction, expressed by Augustine, that while all Scripture was given for the edification of the Church and the nurture of the three theological virtues of faith, hope, and love, not all stories in the Bible are edifying as they stand. What is the spiritual point of the story of the drunkenness of Noah, the murder of Sisera, or the oxgoad of Shamgar, son of Anath? If it cannot be found on the level of narrative, then it must be found on the level of allegory, metaphor, and type.

That is not to say that patristic and medieval interpreters approved of arbitrary and undisciplined exegesis, which gave free rein to the imagination of the exegete. Augustine argued, for example, that the more obscure parts of Scripture should be interpreted in the light of its less difficult sections and that no allegorical interpretation could be accepted that was not approved by the "manifest testimonies" of other less ambiguous portions of the Bible. The literal sense of Scripture is basic to the spiritual and limits the range of possible allegorical meanings in those instances in which the literal meaning of a particular passage is absurd, undercuts the living relationship of the Church to the Old Testament, or is spiritually barren.

From the time of John Cassian, the Church subscribed to a theory of the fourfold sense of Scripture.[7] The literal sense of Scripture could and usually did nourish the three theological virtues, but when it did not, the exegete could appeal to three additional senses, each sense corresponding to one of the virtues. The allegorical sense taught about the Church and what it should believe, and so it corresponded to the virtue of faith. The tropological sense taught about individuals and what they should do, and so it corresponded to the virtue of love. The analogical sense pointed to the future and awakened expectation, and so it corresponded to the virtue of hope. In the fourteenth century Nicholas of Lyra summarized this hermeneutical theory in a much quoted little rhyme:

Littera gesta docet,
Quid credas allegoria,
Moralis quid agas,
Quo tendas anagogia.

(The letter teaches stories,
Allegory teaches what to believe,
The moral sense what to do,
Anagogy where to aim for.)

This hermeneutical device made it possible for the Church to pray directly and without qualification even a troubling Psalm like 137. After all, Jerusalem was not merely a city in the Middle East; it was, according to the allegorical sense, the Church; according to the tropological sense, the faithful soul; and according to the anagogical sense, the center of God's new creation. The psalm became a lament of those who long for the establishment of God's future kingdom and who are trapped in this disordered and troubled world, which with all its delights is still not their home. They seek an abiding city elsewhere. The imprecations against the Edomites and the Babylonians are transmuted into condemnations of the world, the flesh, and the devil. If you grant the fourfold sense of Scripture, David sings like a Christian.

Thomas Aquinas wanted to ground the spiritual sense of Scripture even more securely in the literal sense than it had been grounded in patristic thought. Returning to the distinction between "things" and "signs" made by Augustine in *De doctrina Christiana* (though Thomas preferred to use the Aristotelian terminology of "things" and "words"), Thomas argued that while words are the signs of things, things designated by words can themselves be signs of other things. In all merely human sciences, words alone have a sign-character. But in Holy Scripture, the things designated by words can themselves have the character of a sign. The literal sense of Scripture has to do with the sign-character of words; the spiritual sense of Scripture has to do with the sign-character of things. By arguing this way, Thomas was able to show that the spiritual sense of Scripture is always based on the literal sense and derived from it.

Thomas also redefined the literal sense of Scripture as "the meaning of the text which the author intends." Lest Thomas be confused with Jowett, I should hasten to point out that for Thomas the author was God, not the human prophet or apostle. In the fourteenth century, Nicholas of Lyra, a Franciscan exegete and one of the most impressive biblical scholars produced by the Christian Church, built a new hermeneutical theory on the aphorism of Thomas. If the literal sense of Scripture is the meaning that the author intended (presupposing that the author whose intention finally matters is God), then is it possible to argue that Scripture contains a double literal sense? Is there a literal-historical sense (the original meaning of the words as spoken in their first historical setting) that includes and implies a literal-prophetic sense (the larger meaning of the words as perceived in later and changed circumstances)?

Nicholas not only embraced a theory of the double literal sense of Scripture, but he was even willing to argue that in certain contexts the literal-prophetic sense takes precedence over the literal-historical. Commenting on Psalm 117, Lyra wrote: "The literal sense in the Psalm concerns Christ; for the literal sense is the sense primarily intended by the author." Of the promise to Solomon in I Chronicles 17:13, Lyra observed: "The aforementioned authority was literally fulfilled in Solomon; however, it was fulfilled less perfectly, because Solomon was a son of God only by grace; but it was fulfilled more perfectly in Christ, who is the Son of God by nature."

For most exegetes, the theory of Nicholas of Lyra bound the interpreter to the dual task of explaining the historical meaning of a text while elucidating its larger and later spiritual significance. The great French humanist, Jacques Lefèvre d'Etaples, however, pushed the theory to absurd limits. He argued that the only possible meaning of a text was its literal-prophetic sense and that the literal-historical sense was a product of human fancy and idle imagination. The literal-historical sense is the "letter that kills." It is advocated as the true meaning of Scripture only by carnal persons who have not been regenerated by the life-giving Spirit of God. The problem of the proper exegesis of Scripture is, when all is said and done, the problem of the regeneration of its interpreters.

In this brief survey of medieval hermeneutical theory, there are certain dominant themes that recur with dogged persistence. Medieval exegetes admit that the words of Scripture had a meaning in the historical situation in which they were first uttered or written, but they deny that the meaning of the words is restricted to what the human author thought he said or what his first audience thought they heard. The stories and sayings of Scripture bear an implicit meaning only understood by a later audience. In some cases that implicit meaning is far more important than the restricted meaning intended by the author in his particular cultural setting.

Yet the text cannot mean anything a later audience wants it to mean. The language of the Bible opens up a field of possible meanings. Any interpretation that falls within that field is valid exegesis of the text, even though that interpretation was not intended by the author. Any interpretation that falls outside the limits of that field of possible meanings is probably eisegesis and should be rejected as unacceptable. Only by confessing the multiple sense of Scripture is it possible for the Church to make use of the Hebrew Bible at all or to recapture the various levels of significance in the unfolding story of creation and redemption. The notion that Scripture has only one meaning is a fantastic idea and is certainly not advocated by the biblical writers themselves.

II

Having elucidated medieval hermeneutical theory, I should like to take some time to look at medieval exegetical practice. One could get the impression from Jowett that because medieval exegetes rejected the theory of the single meaning of Scripture so dear to Jowett's heart, they let their exegetical imaginations run amok and exercised no discipline at all in clarifying the field of possible meanings opened by the biblical text. In fact, medieval interpreters, once you grant the presuppositions on which they operate, are as conservative and restrained in their approach to the Bible as any comparable group of modern scholars.

In order to test medieval exegetical practice I have chosen a terribly difficult passage from the Gospel of Matthew, the parable of the good employer or, as it is more frequently known, the parable of the workers in the vineyard (Matt. 20:1-16). The story is a familiar one. An employer hired day laborers to work in his vineyard at dawn and promised them the standard wage of a denarius. Because he needed more workers, he returned to the marketplace at nine, noon, three, and five o'clock and hired any laborers he could find. He promised to pay the workers hired at nine, noon, and three what was fair. But the workers hired at the eleventh hour or five o'clock were sent into the vineyard without any particular promise concerning remuneration. The employer instructed his foreman to pay off the workers beginning with the laborers hired at five o'clock. These workers expected only one-twelfth of a denarius, but were given the full day's wage instead. Indeed, all the workers who had worked part of the day were given one denarius. The workers who had been in the vineyard since dawn accordingly expected a bonus beyond the denarius, but they were disappointed to receive the same wage that had been given to the other, less deserving workers. When they grumbled, they were told by the employer that they had not been defrauded but had been paid according to an agreed contract. If the employer chose to be generous to the workers who had only worked part of the day, that was, in effect, none of their business. They should collect the denarius that was due them and go home like good fellows.

Jesus said the kingdom of God was like this story. What on earth could he have meant?

The Church has puzzled over this parable ever since it was included in Matthew's Gospel. Thomas Aquinas in his *Lectura super Evangelium Sancti Matthaei* offered two interpretations of the parable, one going back in its lineage to Irenaeus and the other to Origen. The "day" mentioned in the parable can either refer to the life-span of an individual (the tradition of Origen), in which case the parable is a comment on the various ages at which one may be converted to Christ, or it is a reference to the history of salvation (the tradition of Irenaeus), in which case it is a comment on the relationship of Jew and Gentile.

If the story refers to the life-span of a man or woman, then it is intended as an encouragement to people who are converted to Christ late in life. The workers in the story who begin at dawn are people who have served Christ and have devoted themselves to the love of God and neighbor since childhood. The other hours mentioned by Jesus refer to the various stages of human development from youth to old age. Whether one has served Christ for a long time or for a brief moment, one will still receive the gift of eternal life. Thomas

154

qualifies this somewhat in order to allow for proportional rewards and a hierarchy in heaven. But he does not surrender the main point: eternal life is given to late converts with the same generosity it is given to early converts.

On the other hand, the story may refer to the history of salvation. Quite frankly, this is the interpretation that interests Thomas most. The hours mentioned in the parable are not stages in individual human development but epochs in the history of the world from Adam to Noah, from Noah to Abraham, from Abraham to David, and from David to Christ. The owner of the vineyard is the whole Trinity, the foreman is Christ, and the moment of reckoning is the resurrection from the dead. The workers who are hired at the eleventh hour are the Gentiles, whose complaint that no one has offered them work can be interpreted to mean that they had no prophets as the Jews had. The workers who have borne the heat of the day are the Jews, who grumble about the favoritism shown to latecomers, but who are still given the denarius of eternal life. As a comment on the history of salvation, the parable means that the generosity of God undercuts any advantage that the Jews might have had with respect to participation in the gifts and graces of God.

Not everyone read the text as a gloss on Jewish–Christian relations or as a discussion of late conversion. In the fourteenth century, the anonymous author of *The Pearl,* an elegy on the death of a young girl, applied the parable to infancy rather than to old age. What is important about the parable is not the chronological age at which one enters the vineyard, but the fact that some workers are only in the vineyard for the briefest possible moment. A child who dies at the age of two years is, in a sense, a worker who arrives at the eleventh hour. The parable is intended as a consolation for bereaved parents. A parent who has lost a small child can be comforted by the knowledge that God, who does not despise the service of persons converted in extreme old age, does not withhold his mercy from boys and girls whose eleventh hour comes at dawn.

Probably the most original interpretation of the parable was offered by John Pupper of Goch, a Flemish theologian of the fifteenth century, who used the parable to attack the doctrine of proportionality, particularly as that doctrine had been stated and defended by Thomas Aquinas. No one had ever argued that God gives rewards that match in exact quantity the weight of the good works done by a Christian. That is arithmetic equality and is simply not applicable to a relationship in which people perform temporal acts and receive eternal rewards. But most theologians did hold to a doctrine of proportionality; while there is a disproportion between the good works that Christians do and the rewards that they receive, there is a proportion as well. The reward is always much larger than the work that is rewarded, but the greater the work, the greater the reward.

As far as Goch is concerned, that doctrine is sheer nonsense. No one can take the message of the parable of the vineyard seriously and still hold to the doctrine of proportionality. Indeed, the only people in the vineyard who hold to the doctrine of proportionality are the first workers in the vineyard. They argue that twelve times the work should receive twelve times the payment. All they receive for their argument is a rebuke and a curt dismissal.

Martin Luther, in an early sermon preached in 1517 before the Reformation, agreed with Goch that God gives equal reward for great and small works. It is not by the herculean size of our exertions but by the goodness of God that we receive any reward at all. But Luther, unfortunately, spoiled this point by elaborating a thoroughly unconvincing argument in which he tried to show that the last workers in the vineyard were more humble than the first and therefore that one hour of their service was worth twelve hours of the mercenary service of the grumblers.

The parable, however, seems to make exactly the opposite point. The workers who began early were not more slothful or more selfish than the workers who began later in the day. Indeed, they were fairly representative of the kind of worker to be found hanging around the marketplace at any hour. They were angry, not because they had shirked their responsibilities, but because they had discharged them conscientiously.

In 1525 Luther offered a fresh interpretation of the parable, which attacked it from a slightly different angle. The parable has essentially one point: to celebrate the goodness of God that makes nonsense of a religion based on law-keeping and good works. God pays no attention to the proportionately greater efforts of the first workers in the vineyard, but, to their consternation, God puts them on exactly the same level as the last and least productive workers. The parable shows that everyone in the vineyard is unworthy, though not always for the same reason. The workers who arrive after nine o'clock are unworthy because they are paid a salary incommensurate with their achievement in picking grapes. The workers who spent the entire day in the vineyard are unworthy because they are dissatisfied with what God has promised, think that their efforts deserve special consideration, and are jealous of their employer's goodness to workers who accomplish less than they did. The parable teaches that salvation is not grounded in human merit and that there is no system of bookkeeping that can keep track of the relationship between God and human beings. Salvation depends utterly and absolutely on the goodness of God.

The four medieval theologians I have mentioned—Thomas Aquinas, the author of *The Pearl*, the Flemish chaplain Goch, and the young Martin Luther—did not exhaust in their writings all the possible interpretations of the parable of the workers in the vineyard. But they did see with considerable clarity that the parable is an assertion of God's generosity and mercy to people who do not deserve it. It is only against the background of the generosity of God that one can understand the relationship of Jew and Gentile, the problem of late conversion, the meaning of the death of a young child, the question of proportional rewards, even the definition of grace itself. Every question is qualified by the severe mercy of God, by the strange generosity of the owner of the vineyard who pays the non-productive latecomer the same wage as his oldest and most productive employees.

If you were to ask me which of these interpretations is valid, I should have to respond that they all are. They all fall within the field of possible meanings created by the story itself. How many of those meanings were in the conscious intention of Jesus or of the author of the Gospel of Matthew, I do not profess to know. I am inclined to agree with C. S. Lewis, who commented on his own book *Till We Have Faces:* "An author doesn't necessarily understand the meaning of his own story better than anyone else"[8] The act of creation confers no special privileges on authors when it comes to the distinctly different, if lesser task of interpretation. Wordsworth the critic is not in the same league with Wordsworth the poet, while Samuel Johnson the critic towers over Johnson the creative artist. Authors obviously have something in mind when they write, but a work of historical or theological or aesthetic imagination has a life of its own.

III

Which brings us back to Benjamin Jowett. Jowett rejected medieval exegesis and insisted that the Bible should be read like any other book.[9] I agree with Jowett that the Bible should be read like any other book. The question is, How does one read other books?

Take, for example, my own field of Reformation studies. Almost no historian that I know would answer the question of the meaning of the writings of Martin Luther by focusing solely on Luther's explicit and conscious intention. Marxist interpreters of Luther from Friedrich Engels to Max Steinmetz have been interested in Luther's writings as an expression of class interests, while psychological interpreters from Grisar to Erikson have focused on the theological writings as clues to the inner psychic tensions in the personality of Martin Luther. Even historians who reject Marxist and psychological interpretations of Luther find themselves asking how Luther was understood in the free imperial cities, by the German knights, by the landed aristocracy, by the various subgroups of German peasants, by the Catholic hierarchy, by lawyers, by university faculties—to name only a few of the more obvious groups who responded to Luther and left a written record of their response. Meaning involves a listener as well as a speaker, and when one asks the question of the relationship of Luther to his various audiences in early modern Europe, it becomes clear that there was not one Luther in the sixteenth century, but a battalion of Luthers.

Nor can the question of the meaning of Luther's writings be answered by focusing solely on Luther's contemporaries. Luther's works were read and pondered in a variety of historical and cultural settings from his death in 1546 to the present. Those readings of Luther have had measurable historical effects on succeeding generations, whose particular situation in time and space could scarcely have been anticipated by Luther. Yet the social, political, economic, cultural, and religious history of those people belongs intrinsically and inseparably to the question of the meaning of the theology of Martin Luther. The meaning of historical texts cannot be separated from the complex problem of their reception and the notion that a text means only what its author intends it to mean is historically naïve. Even to talk of the original setting in which words were spoken and heard is to talk of meanings rather than meaning. To attempt to understand those original meanings is the first step in the exegetical process, not the last and final step.

Modern literary criticism has challenged the notion that a text means only what its author intends it to mean far more radically than medieval exegetes ever dreamed of doing. Indeed, contemporary debunking of the author and the author's explicit intentions has proceeded at such a pace that it seems at times as if literary criticism has become a jolly game of ripping out an author's shirttail and setting fire to it. The reader and the literary work to the exclusion of the author have become the central literary preoccupation of the literary critic. Literary relativists of a fairly moderate sort insist that every generation has its own Shakespeare and Milton, and extreme relativists loudly proclaim that no reader reads the same work twice. Every change in the reader, however slight, is a change in the meaning of a text. Imagine what Thomas Aquinas or Nicholas of Lyra would have made of the famous statement of Northrop Frye:

It has been said of Boehme that his books are like a picnic to which the author brings the words and

161

the reader the meaning. The remark may have been
intended as a sneer at Boehme, but it is an exact
description of all works of literary art without
exception.[10]

Medieval exegetes held to the sober middle way,
the position that the text (any literary text, but
especially the Bible) contains both letter and spirit.
The text is not all letter, as Jowett and others
maintained, or all spirit, as the rather more
enthusiastic literary critics in our own time are apt to
argue. The original text as spoken and heard limits a
field of possible meanings. Those possible meanings
are not dragged by the hair, willy-nilly, into the text,
but belong to the life of the Bible in the encounter
between author and reader as they belong to the life
of any act of the human imagination. Such a
hermeneutical theory is capable of sober and
disciplined application and avoids the Scylla of
extreme subjectivism, on the one hand, and the
Charybdis of historical positivism, on the other. To
be sure, medieval exegetes made bad mistakes in the
application of their theory, but they also scored
notable and brilliant triumphs. Even at their worst
they recognized that the intention of the author is
only one element—and not always the most important element at that—in the complex phenomenon
of the meaning of a text.

The defenders of the single-meaning theory
usually concede that the medieval approach to the
Bible met the religious needs of the Christian
community, but that it did so at the unacceptable
price of doing violence to the biblical text. The fact
that the historical-critical method after two hundred

years is still struggling for more than a precarious foothold in that same religious community is generally blamed on the ignorance and conservatism of the Christian laity and the sloth or moral cowardice of its pastors.

I should like to suggest an alternative hypothesis. The medieval theory of levels of meaning in the biblical text, with all its undoubted defects, flourished because it is true, while the modern theory of a single meaning, with all its demonstrable virtues, struggles because it is false. Until the historical-critical method becomes critical of its own theoretical foundations and develops a hermeneutical theory adequate to the nature of the text that it is interpreting, it will remain restricted, as it deserves to be, to the guild and the academy, where the question of truth can endlessly be deferred.

NOTES

1. Benjamin Jowett, "On the Interpretation of Scripture," *Essays and Reviews*, 7th ed. (London: Longman, Green, Longman, & Roberts, 1861), pp. 330-433.

2. Ibid., p. 378.

3. Ibid., p. 384.

4. Ibid., p. 412.

5. Helen Gardner, *The Business of Criticism* (London: Oxford University Press, 1959), p. 83.

6. Origen, *On First Principles*, ed. G. W. Butterworth (New York: Harper & Row, 1966), p. 288.

7. For a brief survey of medieval hermeneutical theory that takes into account recent historical research see James S. Preus, *From Shadow to Promise* (Cambridge, Mass.: Harvard University Press, 1969), pp. 9-149; see also the useful bibliography, pp. 287-93.

8. W. H. Lewis, ed., *Letters of C. S. Lewis* (New York: Harcourt, Brace & World, 1966), p. 273.

9. Jowett, "Interpretation," p. 377.

10. This quotation is cited by E. D. Hirsch, Jr., *Validity in Interpretation* (New Haven: Yale University Press, 1967), p. 1, at the beginning of a chapter that sets out to elaborate an alternative theory.

TEN

The Making of a Theologian

The students sitting around the table were talking. At the moment I was doing nothing more than listening. The topic under discussion was the seminary's vision of its task and what the students felt was deficient in that vision.

"You know," one student said, "the seminary is training us to be theologians in residence in the local parish. I'm not sure I buy that image."

"No," chimed in another student, "the faculty doesn't seem to realize that we have rejected them as a model for ministry in the local parish."

"Ministry has to be functional," added still a third. "It has to be structured around the felt needs of people."

I sat at the table, trying to look inscrutable and feeling mystified. Certainly the theological task was not the only function for which these men and women were being trained. But it was by anyone's standards—except the most radical—a central function of the parish ministry. For the next forty years, if these students stick it out, they will talk in public about God, perhaps in elementary terms. But even elementary talk about God is theology.

That is not to say, of course, that there were not reasons I could think of why students might be reluctant to take up the theological task. They had wandered for three years in a wilderness of technical terms and jargon—*Heilsgeschichte,* magisterium, hypostatic union, Christ-event, *ex opere operantis,* new being—much of which they had only understood after a long struggle and all of which is foreign to most parishioners in Springfield or Allentown or Altoona. Their own involvement in the parish had taught them that few people are troubled about the kind of questions that are daily fare in the theological seminary. The parish, after all, is not interested in theological questions; it is interested in theological answers. If a theologian such as Bultmann or Cobb or Reuther has raised a valid theological question but has given what ordinary Christians regard as an inadequate answer, the parish will reject both question and answer.

Of what possible use, then, is a technical theological vocabulary in such a parish? Why struggle to master the tools for critical exegesis when the average layperson still believes that the Pentateuch was written by Moses and rejects the theory of a second (to say nothing of a third) Isaiah. Haven't students been trained in skills they will never be asked to use, and that might very well be opposed if they were used? Isn't it the case that students have been trained for life in the university rather than for life in the world?

It is a fair question and not one that can be shunted aside as anti-intellectual or pietistic. A gap between the seminary and the parish does exist in fact and not simply in the imagination of students. It is a gap that has driven numbers of bright students to reject the parish for the university and that has compelled many compassionate pastors to reject the university and its theology for the parish.

It is a real problem and not an imaginary one. And yet the whole debate seems to me to rest on an indefensible basis. The seminary insists on the necessity and usefulness of certain academic disciplines and is suspicious (with perfect right) of the kind of cheap faith that never troubles itself with questions and that glosses over all the hard problems with a pious "let us pray." There is such a thing as loving God with the mind and any Christian who has not yet come to see that has not grown very far in the Christian faith.

The parish, on the other hand, observes that the mastery of intellectual disciplines is not the same thing as faith and notes (with equally perfect right) that the seminary often harbors the kind of gnostic pride that dispenses with elementary trust in God and risks absolutely nothing, not even tenure, for the kingdom of heaven. We are, after all, justified by faith and not by data. If we are not saved by our contributions to the Community Chest, neither are we redeemed by our contributions to scholarship. Karl Barth's dream of the angels laughing at him while he pulled a little wagon behind him loaded

166

down with his multi-volume dogmatics is the only appropriate attitude of Christian scholars to the works of their own hands. "Angels can fly," as G. K. Chesterton observed, "because they take themselves lightly." Laughter at one's own pretensions is a necessary gift of grace.

The seminary insists that faith must be critical and responsive to the data of the various academic disciplines. The parish insists with no less fervor that Christians are justified by faith and not by mastery of those same disciplines. Both are right in what they affirm and wrong in what they deny. Faith must be critical, but it must be faith; it must take risks for the kingdom of God. Faith must be faith, but it must also be critical; not every risk is a risk we are impelled to take for the sake of the kingdom. It is possible to leap blindly into the lap of the devil as well as into the arms of God. Faith is not credulity and the Bible does not praise the gullible person.

All this is a way of saying that theology is essential to the life of the Church. It is not the case that theology is a bloodless mastery of data or that the calling to engage in theology is antithetical to the calling to commit oneself in faith. Theology is not a neutral discipline like the study of aerodynamics. The subject of theology is not God in himself and not, as Feuerbach thought, human nature in itself. Theology is concerned with God in his relationship of judgment and grace to human beings and human beings in their relationships of disobedience and faith to God.

Luther understood that theology is never reflection about God in himself. The really important thing in theology is that this God stands in a relationship to me. I am touched by him, driven by him to a decision, saved through him. Otherwise I do not theologize but only speculate about religious topics. I could put it this way: theology is applied knowledge, not a pure science interested in things in themselves. Theology is an ellipse with two foci. Where I am not included in my reflections about God, there is no theology but only philosophy of religion. Only insofar as God reveals himself to me, only insofar as I am confronted by this God and my faith is awakened, can theology be engaged in at all. Everything that stands outside the circle of light cast by revelation is impenetrable darkness. Outside revelation I only encounter the threatening riddle of my own existence.

The essence of God consists in the fact that he is my God. I cannot think of the Godhood of God as something unrelated to me. Otherwise I am thinking of a myth or fable. I can only think of God as one who is good to me, as either my judge—the Lord who lays waste about him—or as my merciful Father. Christian theology is reflection in time and therefore time-conditioned about the God who is my God and who has made himself accessible to me in Jesus Christ.

Theology is a practical science. Therefore the mastery of theological disciplines is not theology but only the passageway that leads into the chamber where theology takes place. What makes a theologian is not the conceptual grasp of certain academic disciplines but rather life in the reality toward which those disciplines point and to which they are the door. If the parish is wrong to suggest that students should not submit themselves and their naïve ideas to the crucible of critical reflection, the divinity school is wrong if it suggests that the task of theology has been completed when students have been supplied with certain data and certain skills. I do not become a theologian until my being has been placed in question by the Word of God, until I have been destroyed by the left hand of God's wrath and re-created by the right hand of his mercy. Until then I am a dabbler, but I am not a theologian.

Martin Luther observed that a theologian is made by *meditatio, tentatio, oratio*—meditation, temptation, and prayer. It is a very hard word for us to accept. As sex was a taboo subject for our grandparents, so death and piety are taboo subjects with us. Other generations were afraid of appearing "loose"; we are fearful of being thought either "morbid" or "pious." So we brush that triad of meditation, temptation, and prayer aside as the relic of outdated piety and lose ourselves in yet another book on liberation or in yet another action project. We preoccupy ourselves with the furniture of the antechamber or scurry back through the corridor into what we believe will be the clean air of simple faith or unreflecting action. But it is never possible in the spiritual life to progress by regression to an earlier stage of faith and what does not grow withers and dies.

The walls of the chamber in which theology occurs are inscribed with these words: meditation, temptation, and prayer. They may be ignored but they cannot be bypassed. Eberhard Bethge in his biography of Dietrich Bonhoeffer noted that Bonhoeffer first became a theologian, then a disciple, and finally a contemporary. For Luther all three are bound up in the one word, theologian. Theology is a serious matter in which life itself is at stake, my life as a contemporary human being. So he insisted again and again on the triad of meditation, temptation, and prayer and repeated the text from Sirach 2:1, "My son, if you come forward to serve the Lord, prepare yourself for temptation." There is no way past this triad, only a way through.

1. *Meditation.* Theology begins with the Word of God which has been spoken to us. It is, I think, not an exaggeration to say that we have forgotten how to meditate on the Word of God. Too often we see the biblical text only as a subject for analysis, not as a Word directed toward us and our situation.

In part the difficulty we find in meditation is the result of a loss of naïveté. Naïve faith talks easily in the second person to and about God. Young people around a campfire at the end of a summer conference use easily such terms as "the will of God for my life" and can pray in simple, direct language. At theological school we shift from second to third person. We no longer talk about "the will of God for my life" but about "the implications of the biblical message"—a phrase that has the third person built into it.

We cannot and should not go back to the language of simple faith, which is no longer our language. But neither can we live for very long in the arid land of "he," "she," and "it." We dare not reject the tools of biblical scholarship but we cannot be satisfied merely to polish them. We must use them to fight our way back through the text to the language of personal encounter. We must learn with a critical and not with a naïve faith how to address God once again as "Thou." We must learn to hear the Word in the text that lies before us. With the tools with which we have mastered the text, we must in a new way open ourselves to the mastery of the text over us. Theologians must learn to meditate, to hear the Word of God that is spoken to them.

2. *Temptation.* The Word that is spoken must be appropriated. But it cannot be appropriated without temptation. Temptation is the desire to be unfaithful to God, to resist the Word that is spoken to me. Of course, temptation comes to us in many ways. But the two most dangerous temptations are the temptations to security and to despair.

Ministers are often lulled into a sense of security through a deadening familiarity with the outsides of holy things. Teachers of religion are sometimes seduced by the conviction that people who deal with holy subjects are superior to people who do not, as if chairs of theology are higher than chairs of history or biochemistry. There is a kind of pride in having the truth that has lost its sense of terror in the presence of absolute mystery. There is a kind of gnostic delight in theological knowledge that no longer shrinks in the presence of the judgment of God's law. The demands of the law are demands that we relay to other people but do not feel they are demands on us. God's law is no longer taken seriously as a claim upon our lives. As professional clergy we have a kind of congressional immunity that allows us to legislate for others what we ourselves are free to ignore. The call to lose oneself, to risk all for the kingdom of heaven, is a call to the laity, who, we delight in observing, do not obey it. We dismiss the exhortation to pluck out our own eye or cut off our own hand as so much oriental hyperbole or we engage in theological rationalizations of the absolute claims of the gospel. We sooth our conscience with cheap grace and pronounce absolution upon ourselves without repentance. There is a very dangerous temptation to security.

But there is also an even more dangerous temptation to despair. We forget that God's wrath is his penultimate rather than his final Word. We overlook the fact that underneath God's no is a deeply hidden yes. We take God's demands with such seriousness that we forget his promises. We are so crushed by the ethical demands of the kingdom that we forget that we are never justified by the purity of our response but only by faith.

The most common form of pastoral despair is despair over the Church. We observe in the Bible that the Church is an army and forget that it is a hospital as well. Therefore we are disillusioned when the Church does not march to the battle but only, somewhat belatedly, hobbles there on crutches.

There is a heresy abroad in the land that the Church is well and knows what the gospel is and has only to apply that gospel to the world, a world that has come of age and is so independent of the moral tutelage of the Church that it does not see why it needs to hear the gospel. But the Church is not well. The whole have no need of a physician but only the sick—and the Church is filled with the sick and wounded. Moreover, the natural tendency of the parish, any parish, is toward faithlessness. It will abandon the gospel if given half a chance and must be reminded over and over again by Word and sacrament what demands have been laid on it by God and what has been given to it in the gospel. We have a desperate need in our time for the proclamation of the sovereign grace of God to the Church. I do not hear the grace of God proclaimed in the churches I visit—only works-righteousness—and I do not have the feeling that my experience is unique.

Protestants, as the late Gustave Weigel once remarked, are always rebelling against their grandparents. Protestants are peculiarly prone to iconoclasm and to the mistaken belief that it is possible to begin *de novo*. That much of what the average Protestant parish does is irrelevant to the needs of the world and that the local congregation is in need of reformation I willingly admit. But I have also not forgotten that it was in precisely that kind of imperfect parish that I was confronted with the reality of God through the gospel. We must, I am afraid, in all our zeal for reformation learn to have a little patience with ambiguity. The genuineness of the Church's confession, which is real, is hidden under the ambiguity of its sin. The Church is just and sinful alike. It is not one or the other; it is both at once. It is the sensitive soul, who does not really understand justification by faith and who divides the world into right and wrong, into just and unjust, who will always be in despair over the Church. The hope that the gospel affords is a hope in spite of the Church, not because of it.

3. Prayer. I must reply to the Word of God that is spoken to me and that I am always tempted to dispute or abandon. I remember one of the students in Drew Theological Seminary came back with a question that had been posed to him during a hospital visit. If God knows all our needs before we pray, so ran the question, why pray? That question stumped the fourth floor of Hoyt-Bowne dormitory. Clearly God was some kind of heavenly quartermaster. If all our requisitions were known in advance, why should we fill out our own requisition forms and submit them through channels.

Luther posed a similar question in the Smaller Catechism. Why do we pray that God's kingdom come, his will be done, even though his kingdom will come whether we pray for its coming or not. Luther responded that we pray that it will come to us, that we will be included in its coming. God is working his purpose in history whether we are in on it or not. But we pray that we may be included.

Prayer is not the submission of a series of requests. It is, to use a well-worn word, a dialogue, a personal encounter and communion. God has spoken our name: "Adam, where art thou?" Prayer is response to the Word spoken to us and unless we respond, the Word is spoken in vain.

Theologians are not made by seminaries, though seminaries lay the necessary foundation. They are made by meditation, temptation, and prayer. Therefore, we are not yet but are only in the process of becoming theologians. We are like the ten-year-old boy who has inherited his sixteen-year-old brother's clothing. The trousers belong to us but they do not yet fit. Our conceptual reach has exceeded our experiential grasp. We must grow into the faith that we profess.

"My son [or daughter], if you come forward to serve the Lord, prepare yourself for temptation." There is no way around this salutary testing, only a way through.

DATE DUE

HIGHSMITH   #LO-45220